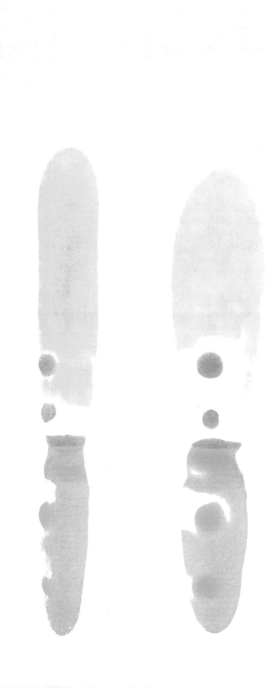

ISLAM IN AFRICA SOUTH OF THE SAHARA

ISLAM IN AFRICA
SOUTH OF THE SAHARA

A select bibliographic guide

Patrick E. Ofori

University of Cape Coast

1977
KTO PRESS
Nendeln

ISBN 3-262-00003-5

Printed in the Netherlands

Dedicated to

Nana Ama & Kofi Boateng

CONTENTS

ACKNOWLEDGEMENTS

I am grateful to the Board of Trustees of the Authorship Development Fund for their grant which made it possible for me to travel within Ghana to collect material for this project.

I am, once again, indebted to Mr. E.K. Koranteng, University Librarian, who suggested to me to undertake this compilation and gave me the necessary support and encouragement.

I wish to express my indebtedness to the various authors and publishers whose works have been quoted or referred to in the introduction to this work. My sincere thanks go to my colleagues, Dr. S.Y. Boadi-Siaw, Messrs Kwaku Amoabeng and Kwabena Amponsah for their assistance during the compilation of this bibliography.

Finally, my thanks go to Mr. Victor F. Gbadagba of the University Printing Press for the skill with which he typed this manuscript.

P.E.O.

INTRODUCTION

This bibliography is the last in a series of three subject bibliographies intended by the compiler to cover aspects of religion in Africa, south of the Sahara. The first volume covered the literature on Black African traditional religions and philosophy. The second volume covered the literature on Christianity in tropical Africa. This third volume covers the literature on Islam in Africa South of the Sahara. With the publication of this last volume the compiler's aim of providing biblio- graphic guides to cover the three competing religions of Africa, namely, Traditional, Christian and Islamic religions has been achieved. The study of these three religions has occupied the attention of many scholars for over four centuries, and the increasing importance of religious studies is manifested in the wide range of literature covered in the previous bibliographies and in the present volume.

The early contact of Islam with Africa began during the life time of the Prophet Muhammed. It is recorded that the prophet himself encouraged the first batch of Muslims who were being persecuted by the Quaraishites in Arabia to migrate to Abyssinia, where they sought refuge under Negus, a Christian King of Abyssinia, in the year 615 A.D. By 639 A.D., the first Muslim volunteer force, under the command of Amr Ibn Al'As, penetrated into Egypt. However, the first serious attempt to expand Islam in Africa is credited to Ugba Ibn Nafi, who after the conquest of Ifriqiya, (The Maghreb), established a permanent camp at Qayrawan in 670 A.D., and undertook the spread of the Islamic faith into Africa and Spain.

Islam first reached the Savannah region of the Sudan

1

in the 8th century, the date from which the written
history of West Africa begins. Muslim historians began
to write about West Africa early in the 8th century.
Ibn Munabbah, a famous Arabic scholar, wrote as early as
738 A.D., and was followed in 947 A.D. by Al-Masudi. The
spread of Islam in the Savannah region was followed by
the establishment of commercial links with North Africa.
Trade and commerce paved the way for the introduction of
new elements of Islamic culture, which made possible the
spread of literacy and intellectual development. Centres
of Islamic learning, such as those of Timbuctu and Jenne
in West Africa helped to produce scholarly religious and
historical literature in Arabic.

By the year 850 A.D. Islam had been accepted in the
Kingdom of Tekrur by the Dya'ogo dynasty. This dynasty
was the first negro kingdom to accept Islam, and for
this reason the Arab historians referred to it as Bilad
al-Tekrur or the ''land of the Black Muslims.''

Eminent Arab historians like Al-Bakri, Al-Masudi,
Ibn Batuta and Ibn Khaldun have written about the glories
of the Bilad as Sudan, ''the land of the Blacks.'' It is
generally acknowledged by historians that the great
medieval empires such as Ghana, Mali, Songhay and Kanem
Bornu rose to the apogee of their glory and power through
their connection with Islamic traders and scholars.

The earliest account of the medieval Ghana empire
was recorded by Al-Bakri, a famous Muslim geographer, in
his book, Kitab tl Masalik wal Mamlik in 1068. According
to Al-Bakri, the King of Ghana at that time employed
muslim interpreters; and most of his Ministers and
Treasurers were also Muslims. These Muslim ministers
were learned in Arabic, and were able to correspond in
the Arabic language which made it possible to establish

diplomatic relations with the Islamic world. The Ghana empire came to an end in 1076, following its conquest by the Almoravids, a militant Muslim movement which originated among the nomadic Berber tribes of the Sanhaja.

The empire of Mali rose from the ruins of the old Ghana empire. The influence of Islam in Mali dates from the 14th century when its Muslim ruler, Mansa Musa, made a successful pilgrimage to Mecca in 1324-25 and brought with him a number of Muslim scholars and Architects who built mosques. Muslim scholars and traders contributed enormously to the cultural and economic development of Mali, the name of the country appearing for the first time on the map of the world during the reign of Mansa Musa.

Islam began to spread into the Songhay empire in the 13th century during the reign of the Dia dynasty. Askia Muhammad of Songhay made a pilgrimage to Mecca in the year 1497 and was given the title of the 'Khalifa' of the western Sudan.

Islam was accepted for the first time in Kanem-Borun during the reign of Umme-Jilmi who ruled between 1085 and 1097. Kanem became the principal focus of Muslim influence in the central Sudan. By the 13th century a reputable centre of Islamic learning had been established and diplomatic relations were established with Tuat and Tunis.

The spread of Islam into Western Africa was accelerated by the acceptance of the religion in the Hausa states in the early 14th century. The Islamic religion became firmly rooted in Kano during the reign of Muhammad Rumfa (1453-1499), and it became the predominant religion in Northern Nigeria after the jihads of Uthman Dan Fodio in 1804. These jihads had been waged to introduce a

3

revivalist movement into Islam in the Hausa states, and
to remove all syncretic practices. Following the success
of these jihads great Islamic empires florished in the
Hausa states in the 19th century.

Most historians attribute the success of the Islamic
expansion into the interior of Africa to the hard work
and devotion of muslim traders and peripatetic missionaries. However, historical evidence clearly reveals the
fact that the conversion of substantial portions of
Africa, especially in West Africa, came about primarily
as a result of sustained military-religious campaigns in
the form of jihads.

The process of Islamic expansion into the interior
of Africa was facilitated by a number of factors. In
the first place, the agents of islamization who carried
the religion into the interior of Africa, whether Berbers
or black Africans, were ethnically, indigenous Africans.
Secondly, this indigenous factor was responsible to some
extent for the relative political calm and independence
of the early muslim states.

The penetration of Islam into the East coast of
Africa dates back to the 7th century, and it provides
interesting contrast to that of Western and Central
Africa. In East Africa Islam never reached very far
into the interior. Neither did it affect the lives of
as many indigenous Africans as was the case in West
Africa. Secondly, in East Africa Islam remained essen-
tially an Arab religion. Almost all Africans who were
converted to Islam were ipso facto Arabized or absorbed
into the mixed Swahilili community.

Islam today claims over fifty million adherents in
black Africa. Some two thirds of the total sub-Saharan
Muslim population live in West Africa, where Nigeria

4

claims the largest Islamic community, while Senegal, Guinea, Mali and Niger are mainly, though not exclusively Muslim. Smaller Muslim communities are found in Liberia, Ghana and Togo.

In central, eastern and north-eastern Africa, Muslims are in the majority in the northern Sudan, and have virtually no rivals in Zanzibar and the Somali Republic. Islam accounts for about a third of the total population in Ethiopia (especially in Eritrea) and in Tanzania. There are also smaller muslim communities in Kenya, Uganda, Malawi, Zambia and the Congo.

A number of factors account for the rapid expansion of Islam in black Africa. Unlike Christianity, Islam has no stigma attached to it as a Western religion. Islamic adherents accept it as an authentic religion for the black man. In contrast to the early Christian missionaries who lived in seclusion and despised African culture and traditions, the representatives of Islam lived and worked among the African peoples among whom they married and raised families. The concept of Islamic brotherhood is largely accepted among African muslims. Islam more easily fits into the cultural and social framework of the African. African concepts and practices like polygamy and bride price which the Christian missionaries despised are approved by Islam. Islam is at one and the same time a religion, a legal and political entity, and a culture. Islam has been so successful in Africa because in the areas where it has been accepted, it has avoided the distinction between politics and religion and between the church and the state.

From the foregoing analysis, it becomes self-evident that Islam is an important force in Africa, throwing a direct challenge to Christian and traditional religions

in an effort to proselytise the African. As a result
of the great influence of Islamic scholars on the history
of Africa, it has become inevitable that any serious and
objective study of the African past cannot be undertaken
without a knowledge of the Islamic sources of the
literature.

In his review of Vincent Monteil's book L'Islam noir,
Thomas Hodgkins mentions Islam as of major importance in
the scholarly writings on Africa. Islamic studies,
according to Professor Hodgkins, ''throw new light on
the basic problems, or help greatly towards an understanding of the influence of Islam - in past periods of
history and in contemporary situation - on institutions
and ideas in sub-Saharan Africa.''(1)

The importance of Islamic studies in the study of
the African past has been endorsed by C.C. Stewart and
E.K. Stewart in the following quotation:

''Islam is a theme of particular importance to
African historians, largely because where Islam spread
it was generally accompanied by the Arabic script. The
emergence of the Arabic script in the pre-literate
societies of Africa offered one of the most productive
sources for the documentation of the African past.''(2)

It is precisely with the objective of making the
sources of the literature on African Islamic studies
accessible to the scholar and the African historian that
the compilation of this bibliography was undertaken.

----

(1)   Christopher Allen & R.W. Johnson: African perspec-
       tives, Cambridge, 1970. p.3.

(2)   Islam and social order in Mauritania. Oxford,
       1973.

Unfortunately, however, the compiler's ignorance of the Arabic script has not made it possible to include a wide range of manuscript and unpublished materials in the original Arabic script. Such a limitation, no doubt, makes the short comings of the present bibliography very obvious to the Arabic scholar. However, in spite of this limitation, my main aim in compiling this work has been to bring together into a single volume the litera-ture on the Islamic religion in Africa that has been published in European languages since Ibn Batuta's, Travels, A.D. 1325-1354.

The growing interest of scholars in African and Islamic studies makes it desirable that bibliographic guides such as the present one be available in large numbers to help Librarians and scholars to select the relevant documents and materials which are required for serious study and research. Hitherto most bibliographies on African studies concentrated on a particular country or region in Africa. Subject or topical bibliographies on Africa have been rare, or, scanty in the few subject areas where such works exist. It is in this light that these bibliographies on the traditional, Christian and Islamic religions in Africa should be seen as a positive contribution to this area of African studies.

This bibliography has been arranged for the conve-nience of the user. It is arranged under the following headings:- Reference works and bibliographies, General works on Islam, Islam in Africa (General), Islam in the Western Sudan, with a section on the Almoravids and the Almohads because of the importance of these movements in the spread of Islam in the western Sudan. After these headings, the arrangement is by broad geographical areas, namely:- Western, Central, Eastern and Southern

Africa. Under each broad geographical area the arrangement is alphabetical by name of countries. Under each
country division the arrangement is alphabetical by the
name of the author, or, by title in the case of annony-
mous publications. Material listed includes books,
pamphlets, periodical articles, theses and unpublished
dissertations and mimeographed monographs.

The publications listed are mainly in European
languages. Arabic scripts are deliberately ommited
because of the compiler's ignorance of the Arabic
language and the problem of transliteration. As far as
possible, full details for every entry is given where
the information is easily accessible. Details provided
for each entry include the author's name, title, edition,
place of publication, publisher, date of publication,
pagination and bibliographical references, A simple
alphabetical author and name index has also been provided.
Every entry is numbered. The index entries refer to the
item numbers.

P.E.O.

University Library
Cape Coast
1976

REFERENCE WORKS AND BIBLIOGRAPHIES

1. ABD al-RAHMAN Ibn ABD ALLAH, al-SA'DF.
   Documents arabes relatifs a l'histoire du Soudan:
   Tarikh es-Soudan. Edité par O. Houdas avec la
   collaboration de E. Benoist. Paris, Maisonneuve,
   1964.

2. ARIF, Aida S. and ABU HAKIMA, A.M.
   Descriptive catalogue of Arabic manuscripts in
   Nigeria (in the) Jos Museum and Luggard Hall
   Library, Kaduna. London, Luzac, 1965.

3. BECKER, C.H.
   ''Materialien zur kenntnis des Islam in Deutsch-
   Ostafrika.'' Der Islam, v.2, 1911: p.1-48.

4. BECKER, C.H. and MARTIN, B.G.
   ''Materials for the understanding of Islam in
   German East Africa.'' Tanzania Notes and Records,
   v.68, February 1968: p.31-61.

5. BIVAR, A.D.H.
   ''Arabic documents of Northern Nigeria.''
   Bulletin of the School of Oriental and African
   Studies, v.22, 1959: p.324-349.

6. BIVAR, A.D.H. and HISKET, M.
   ''The Arabic literature of Nigeria to 1804: a
   provisional account.'' Bulletin of the School of
   Oriental and African Studies, v.25, 1962: p.104-148.
   A bibliographic essay, containing facsimile
   reproductions of early Arabic writings on Nigeria.

7. BOYO, al-Hajj Eshaka (and others)
    Checklist of Arabic works from Ghana, compiled by
    al-Hajj Osman Eshaka Boyo, Thomas Hodgkin and Ivor
    Wilks. Legon, Institute of African Studies,
    University of Ghana, 1962.

8. BRASSEUR, Paule
    Bibliographie generale du Mali (anciens Soudan
    francais et Haut Senegal-Niger). Dakar, I.F.A.N.,
    1964.

9. _____,
    Les sources bibliographiques de l'Afrique de
    l'ouest d'expression francaise. Dakar, Archives
    Nationales, 1967.

10. BROWN, W.A.
    ''A new bibliographical aid: the Izalat al-Raib
    of Ahmad Abul-I'raf al-Tinbukti.'' In The
    Northern (Nigerian) History Research Scheme.
    Second Interim Report (Zaria, 1967). Also in
    Research Bulletin (Centre of Arabic Documentation,
    Ibadan). v.3, No.2, July 1967: p.129-138.

11. CARSON, Patricia
    Materials for West African history in the archives
    of Belgium and Holland. London, London University
    Press, 1962.

12. _____,
    Materials for West African history in French
    archives. London, The Athlone Press, 1968.

13. CARSON, P. and FEINBERG, H.M.

    ''Further additions to Materials for West African history in the archives of Belgium and Holland.'' African Studies Bulletin, v.12, No.1, April 1969: p.81-89.

14. CENTRE DES HAUTES ETUDES ADMINISTRATIVES SUR L'AFRIQUE ET L'ASIE MODERNES.

    Carte des religions de l'Afrique noire. Republique Islamique de Mauritanie. Paris, C.H.E.A.M., 1960.

15. CONFERENCE ON ARABIC DOCUMENTS, UNIVERSITY OF GHANA. 1965.

    Report. Legon, Institute of African Studies, University of Ghana, 1965.

16. DESTAING, E.

    ''Notes sur les manuscrits arabes de l'Afrique occidentale.'' Revue Africaine, v.55, 1911: p.64-99, 216-248, 484-522. v.56, 1912: p.267-300, 447-469. v.57, 1913: p.139-162.

17. DEVERDUN, G.

    ''Un nouveau manuscrit des Masalik al—Absar d'Ibn Fadi-Allah al—Umari.'' Hesperis, v.41, 1954: p.457-462.

18. DIALLO, T. (and others) (eds.)

    Catalogue des manuscrits de l'IFAN par T. Diallo, B. M'Backe, M. Trifovie et B. Barry. Dakar, IFAN, 1967. (Collection Catalogues et Documents no. 20).

19. DOZY, R.P.A.

Notices sur quelques manuscrits arabes. Leyden,
E.J. Brill, 1847-1851.

20. ENCYCLOPEDIE DE L'ISLAM

Dictionnaire geographique, ethnographique et
biographique des peuples musulmans. Leiden,
Paris, E.J. Brill, t.4 1913 à 1936.

21. The ENCYCLOPAEDIA of Islam: a dictionary of the
geography, ethnography and biography of the
Muhammedan peoples: prepared by a number of
leading orientalists. Edited by M. Th. Houtsma,
A.J. Wensinck, T.W. Arnold, H. Basset and
A. Schaade. London, Luzac: Leyden, Brill, 1925.
1926- 3 vols.

22. FISHER, Humphrey J.

''Three further manuscripts of c Abdullah
b. Fudi's Tazyin al-Waraqat.'' Research Bulletin
(Centre of Arabic Documentation, Univ. of Ibadan).
v.5, No.1/2, December 1969: p.47-56.

23. GRAY, Richard and CHAMBERS, D.S.

Materials for West African history in Italian
archives. London, University of London, Athlone
Press, 1965.

24. HAZARD, Harry W.

Atlas of Islamic history. Princeton, Princeton
University Press, 1951.

25. HISKETT, Mervyn
     ''Materials relating to the state of learning
     among the Fulani before their jihad.'' Bulletin
     of the School of Oriental and African Studies,
     v.19, No.3, 1957: p.550-578.
     Based on original manuscripts in the author's
     possession collected for him in Sokoto by Mallam
     Abubakar Gumi of the School of Arabic Studies,
     Kano.

26. HISKETT, M. and BIVAR, A.D.H.
     ''The Arabic literature of Northern Nigeria to
     1804, a provisional account.'' Bulletin of the
     School of Oriental and African Studies, v.25,
     1962: p.104-148. illus.
     The purpose of this essay is to provide a
     convenient introduction to the Arabic literature
     composed in Nigeria and the immediately adjoining
     areas in the period before the commencement of
     the Fulani jihad.

27. HOLT, Peter M.
     ''The archives of the Mahdia.'' Sudan Notes and
     Records, v.36, No.1, June 1955: p.71-80.

28. HUISMAN, A.J.W.
     Les manuscrits arabes dans le monde; une biblio-
     graphie des catalogues. Leiden, E.J. Brill,
     1967.

29. HUNWICK, John O. and HASSAN, I.
     ''Another look at the de Gironcourt papers.''
     Research Bulletin (Centre of Arabic Documentation,
     Ibadan). v.3, No.2, July 1967: p.74-99.

30. HUNWICK, J.O.
    ''Arabic manuscript material bearing on the
    history of the Western Sudan.'' Supplement,
    Bulletin of News, (Historical Society of Nigeria).
    v.7, No.2, 1962: p.1-9.

31. --------,
    ''A collection of MSS belonging to the Kano
    Native Authority.'' Bulletin of News, Historical
    Society of Nigeria, v.7, No.2, 1962. supplement.

32. IBN ISHARKU, Malam Muhammad Salih
    ''Two Sudanese manuscripts of the seventeenth
    century.'' edited by H.R. Palmer. Bulletin of
    the School of Oriental and African Studies, v.3,
    1929: p.541-560.

33. INTERNATIONAL AFRICAN INSTITUTE. London.
    Cumulative bibliography of African studies.
    Boston, G.K. Hall, 1973. 5 vols.
    A reproduction of the card index of the
    Library of the International African Institute.
    Vol.I, which is the Classified Catalogue,
    contains material on Islam in Africa.

34. JEFFREYS, M.D.W.
    ''Two Arabic documents, Diyya s-Sultan and
    Tazyin l-Waraqat.'' African Studies, v.9,
    1950: p.77-85.

35. KENSDALE, W.E.N.
    ''The Arabic manuscript collection of the library
    of the University College of Ibadan, Nigeria.''
    WALA News, v.2, June 1955: p.21-25.

14

36. KENSDALE, W.E.N.
    A catalogue of Arabic manuscripts preserved in
    the University library, Ibadan; 2nd ed. Ibadan,
    University Press, 1958.

37. ————,
    ''Field notes on the Arabic literature of the
    Western Sudan: Abdullahi dan Fodio.'' Journal
    of the Royal Asiatic Society, April 1956:
    p.78-80.

38. ————,
    ''Field notes on the Arabic literature of the
    Western Sudan: Muhammadu Bello.'' Journal of
    the Royal Asiatic Society, April 1958: p.53-57.

39. ————,
    ''Field notes on the Arabic literature of the
    Western Sudan: Shehu Usuman dan Fodio.'' Journal
    of the Royal Asiatic Society, October 1955:
    p.162-168.

40. LAST, Murray
    ''Arabic manuscripts in the National Archives,
    Kaduna.'' Research Bulletin, (Centre of Arabic
    Documentation, Ibadan), v.2, No.2, 1966: p.1-10.

41. ————,
    ''Arabic source material and historiography in
    Sokoto since 1864: an outline.'' Research Bulletin
    (Centre of Arabic Documentation, Ibadan), v.1,
    No.3, July 1965: p.1-8.

42. LAST, Murray
        ''Arabic source material and historiography in
        Sokoto to 1864: an outline.'' Research Bulletin
        (Centre of Arabic Documentation, Ibadan). v.1,
        No.2, January 1965: p.3-20.

43. ------,
        ''Interim report by the Research Fellow in Nigerian
        history with a short catalogue of Arabic texts
        preserved on Microfilm at Ahmadu Bello University.''
        In Northern History Research Scheme, first interim
        report, Zaria, February 1966: p.22-55.

44. ------,
        ''The recovery of the Arabic script of the North.''
        In Northern History Research Scheme, second
        interim report, Zaria, April 1967: p.33-70.

45. LEVTZION, N.
        ''Early 19th century Arabic manuscripts from
        Kumasi.'' Transactions of the Historical Society
        of Ghana. v.8, 1965: p.99-119.

46. ------,
        ''A seventeenth-century chronicle by Ibn al-Mukthar
        a critical study of 'Tarikh al Fattash'.''
        Bulletin of the School of Oriental and African
        Studies, v.24, 1971: p.571-593.

47. LEWICKI, T.
        ''External Arabic sources for the history of
        Africa to the South of the Sahara.'' In T.O.
        Ranger, (ed.) Emerging themes in African history.
        Nairobi, East African Publishing House, 1968.

48. MAHMUD, Khalil.
    ''The Arabic collections of Ibadan University
    library.'' Libri, v.19, No.2, 1964: p.97-107.

49. MARTIN, B.G.
    ''Arabic Materials for Ghanaian history.''
    Research Review. (Legon) Institute of African
    Studies, University of Ghana. v.2, No.1, April
    1966: p.74-83.

50. ------,
    ''Five letters from the Tripoli archives.''
    Journal of the Historical Society of Nigeria, v.2,
    No.3, 1962: p.350-373.

51. ------,
    ''A Mahdist document from Futa Jallon.'' Bulletin
    de l'Institut Fondamental d'Afrique Noire, v.25,
    series B, No.1-2, January-April 1963: p.47-65.

52. ------,
    ''Turkish archival sources for West African
    history.'' African Studies Bulletin, v.10, No.3,
    1967: p.59-65.

53. MATTHEWS, Daniel G., ed.
    Current themes in African historical studies: a
    selected bibliographical guide to resources for
    research in African history. Westport, Connecticut,
    Negro Universities Press, 1970. 389p.

54. MAUNY, Raymond.
    ''Bibliographie de l'empire du Mali.'' Notes
    Africaines, v.82, 1959: p.55-56.

55. MAUNY, Raymond
     ''Contribution à la bibliographie de l'histoire
     de l'Afrique noire des origines à 1850.''
     Bulletin de l'Institut Fondamental d'Afrique Noire,
     series B, v.28, No.3/4, 1966: p.927-965.

56. MONTEIL, Vincent
     ''Analyse des 25 documents Arabes des Males de
     Bahia (1835).'' Bulletin de l'Institut Fondamental
     d'Afrique Noire, v.29, series B, No.1/2, 1967:
     p.88-98. illus.

57. ------,
     ''Les manuscrits historiques arabo-africains.''
     Bulletin de l'Institut Fondamental d'Afrique Noire
     (B), v.27, No.3/4, 1965: p.531-542, v.28, No.3/4,
     1966: p.668-675, v.29, No.3/4, 1967: p.599-603.

58. el-NAGER, O.A.
     ''A note on the material for the study of Rabah's
     career.'' Bulletin of the African Studies Asso-
     ciation of the United Kingdom, No.6, November
     1965: p.20-23.

59. ODOOM, K.O. and HOLDEN, J.J.
     ''Arabic collection (short description of some
     manuscripts held at the Institute that have
     already been catalogued: a regular feature).''
     Legon, Institute of African Studies, University
     of Ghana, Research Review, v.4, No.1, 1967: p.30-73

60. OULD HAMIDOUN, Mokhtar and HEYMOWSKI, Adam
    Catalogue des manuscrits mauritaniens en langue
    arabe preservés en Mauritanie. Repertoire confe-
    ctionne à la Bibliotheque Nationale de Mauritannie,
    December 1964 à Fevrier 1965: xerographie à la
    Bibliotheque royale de Suede, Stockholm, 1965-1966.

61. PALMER, Sir Herbert Richmond.
    ''Two Sudanese manuscripts of the seventeenth
    century.'' Bulletin of the School of Oriental
    and African Studies, v.5, 1928-1930: p.541-560.

62. PEARSON, J.D.
    Index Islamicus: a catalogue of articles on Islamic
    subjects in periodicals and other collective publi-
    cations (in Western and Russian languages).
    Cambridge Heffer, 1958.   897p.

63. ------,
    Index Islamicus, supplement 1956-1960.   Cambridge,
    Heffer, 1962.   316p.

64. ''QUATRIEME notice d'un manuscrit arabe contenant la
    description de l'Afrique.''   In Notices et extraits
    des Manuscrits à la Bibliotheque du Roi et autre
    bibliotheques.   Paris, 1831.

65. REHFISCH, F.
    ''A note on contemporary source-materials of the
    Sudanese Mahdia.''   Sudan Notes & Records, v.44,
    1963: p.143.

66. RYDER, A.F.C.
    Materials for West African history in Portuguese
    Archives.   London, Athlone Press, 1965.

67. SHORTER encyclopaedia of Islam, edited on behalf of
      the Royal Netherlands Academy by H.A.R. Gibb and
      J.H. Kramers. Leiden, E.J. Brill: Lauzac & Co.,
      1961. v.111, 671p.

68. SMITH, H.F.C.
      ''Arabic manuscript material bearing on the history
      of the Western Sudan.'' Bulletin of News, Historica
      Society of Nigeria. v.4, No.2, 1959: p.1-20
      (supplement).

69. ------,
      ''The Archives of Segu.'' Bulletin of News,
      Historical Society of Nigeria. v.4, No.2, 1959,
      supplement.

70. ------,
      ''A list (published in the 1850s) of books written
      by the Kalifu Muhammad Bello.'' Bulletin of News,
      Historical Society of Nigeria, v.3, No.4, 1959,
      supplement.

71. ------,
      ''An old manuscript from Timbuktu.'' Bulletin of
      News, Historical Society of Nigeria, v.4, No.4,
      March 1960.

72. ------,
      ''Source material for the history of the Western
      Sudan.'' Journal of the Historical Society of
      Nigeria, v.1, No.3, 1958: p.238-248.

73. STERN, S.M. ed.
      Documents from Islamic chanceries. Oxford, Bruno
      Cassirer, London, Faber & Faber, 1968.

74. STEWART, C.

''Notes on North and West African manuscript
material relating to the West African Qadiriyya
tariqa.'' Research Bulletin (Centre of Arabic
Documentation, Univ. of Ibadan). v.4, Nos. 1/2,
December 1968: p.1-25.

75. STRUCK, Bernhard

''A sketch map of Islam in Africa in 1912.''
International Review of Missions, October 1912.

76. TRITTON, A.S.

Materials on Muslim education in the Middle Ages.
London, Luzac, 1957.

77. TAPIERO, Norbert

''Concerning an Arabic manuscript of Sudanese
origin preserved in the Bibliotheque Nationale,
Paris.'' Research Bulletin, (Centre for Arabic
Documentation, Univ. of Ibadan). v.4, Nos. 1/2,
December 1968: p.26-40.

78. UNITED STATES. Library of Congress. African Section.

Africa south of the Sahara: Index to periodical
literature, 1900-1970. Boston, G.K. Hall, 1971.
4 vols.

79. VAJDA, G.

Index general des manuscrits arabes musulmans de
la Bibliotheque Nationale de Paris. Paris,
Editions du C.N.R.S., 1953.

80. ------,

''Notes sur la Geschichte der arabischen literatu:

80. VAJDA, G. (Contd.)

de C. Brockelmam.'' Journal Asiatique, v.238,
1950: p.225-236, v.240, 1952: p.1-36.

81. WAGNER, E.
''Three Arabic documents on the history of Harar.''
Journal of Ethiopian Studies, v.12, No.1, January
1974: p.213-224.

82. WHITTING, C.E.J.
''The unprinted indigenous Arabic literature of
Northern Nigeria.'' Journal of the Royal Asiatic
Society, April 1943.

83. WILKS, Ivor
''A note on the Arabic manuscript IASAR/298, and
others from Wa.'' Research Review, (Legon) v.2,
No.2, 1966: p.63-68.

This manuscript is a short Arabic work on the
sultanate of the town of Wa in North-western
Ghana. It demonstrates that the Wa literary
tradition goes back to at least the earlier 19th
century.

84. YOUNG, Crawford
''Materials for the study of Islam in the Congo.''
Cahiers Economiques et Sociaux, v.4, No.4, Decembe
1966: p.461-464.

Annotated bibliography of Islam in Congo-Kinsha
(Zaire). Divided into four parts (1) the Swahili
states of the 19th century, (2) the Mahdist movement in the Sudan and its influence in Zandeland,
(3) Muslim of Maniema and Stanleyville, (4) the
Muslim community in Leopoldville.

85. ABU BAKR EFFENDI
The religious duties of Islam as taught and
explained by Abu Bakr Effendi. A translation
from the original Arabic and Afrikaans. Edited
with an introduction and notes by Mia Brandel-
Syrier. Leiden, E.J. Brill, 1960. 196p. (Pretoria
Oriental series).

86. ABUN-NASIR, Jamil M.
The Tijaniyya: a sufi order in the modern world.
London, Royal Institute for International Affairs,
1965. 216p.

87. ADDISON, James Thayer
The Christian approach to the Moslem; a historical
study. New York, AMS Press, 1966. 365p.
    A historical survey of the missionary efforts
of the Christian Church to approach the Moslem,
from the beginnings to the present time. Chapter
XV includes efforts made in Negro Africa in this
direction.

88. AHMAD, Mirza Bashir-ud-Deen M.
Why I believe in Islam. (a broadcast talk - Bombay
station, 19th February 1940). Lagos, Islamic
Literature, 1951. 7p.

89. ------,
The preaching of Islam. Rabwah, Ahmadiyya Muslim
Missions, 1964: 34p. illus.

90. AHMAD, Mirza Mubarak

The propagation of Islam: a short account of the
achievements of Tahrik-i-jadid in the cause of
Islam. Rabwah, Ahmadiyya Muslim Missions, 1964.
19p. illus.

91. ALI, Muhammad

The religion of Islam: a comprehensive discussion
of the sources, principles and practices of Islam.
Lahore, Ahmadiyyah Anjuman Ishaat Islam, 1950.

92. AMIR, Ali M.S.

Mahommedan law, compiled from authorities in the
original Arabic. 3rd ed., Calcutta, Thacker,
Spink, 1901-1908. 2 vols. (Tagore law lectures,
1884).

93. ------,

The spirit of Islam: a history of the evolution
and ideals of Islam with the life of the prophet.
London, 1952.

94. ANDERSON, James Norman D.

Maliki law of homicide. Zaria, Gaskiya Corpn.,
1959. 17p.

95. ANDRE, Pierre J.

Confreries religieuses musulmanes. Alger; La
Maison du Livre, 1956.

96. ------,

Contributions a l'études des confreries religieuses
musulmanes. Alger, La Maison des livres, 1956. 368p

24

97. ANDRE, Pierre J.
     ''Contribution a l'etude du mouvement Ahmadia.''
     Bulletin de l'Afrique Francaise, January 1924:
     p.20-32.

98. ------
     L'Islam et les races. Paris, Paul Geuthner, 1922.
     2 vols.
         Volume 2 Chapters VIII, IX and XI treat the
     topics ''L'Islam chez les noirs'' ''L'Islam en
     Abyssine'' and ''Le Sutanata de Zanzibar et
     Madagascar.''

99. ARBERRY, Arthur John
     An introduction to the history of Sufism; the Sir
     Abdullah Suhrawardy lectures for 1942. London,
     Longmans, Green, 1943. xx, 84p. (Calcutta. Univer-
     sity. The Sir Abdullah Suhrawardy lectures, 1942).

100. ------
     Revelation and reason in Islam: the Forwood lectures
     for 1956 delivered in the University of Liverpool.
     London, Allen & Unwin, 1957. 121p.

101. ------,
     Sufism, an account of the mystics of Islam. London,
     Allen & Unwin, 1956. 141p. (Ethical and religious
     classics of East and West, no.2).

102. ARBERRY, Arthur John and LANDAU, Rom
     Islam today. London, Faber & Faber, 1943. 258p.
     illus., bibliog.

103. ARNOLD, Sir Thomas
      The preaching of Islam: a history of the propaga-
      tion of the Muslim faith. Lahore, S. Muhamma
      Ashraf, 1964. 508p.

104. AZZAM, Abdel Rahman
      The eternal message of Muhammad. Translated from
      the Arabic by Caesar E. Farah. With an introduc-
      tion by Vincent Shean. New York, The Devin—Adair
      Company, 1964: xxi, 297p.

105. BACHATLY, C.
      ''Document sur pelerinage a Mecque au debut du Xe
      siecle de l'Hegire (907/1501).'' Bulletin de la
      Societe de Geographie d'Egypte (Cairo) v.21, July
      1943: p.23-27.

106. BIJLEFELD, W.A.
      ''Various attitudes towards modernity in the Muslim
      world.'' Orita. v.1, No.2, December 1967: p.39-49.
         ''The purpose of this article is to indicate
      in a brief outline, with all the dangers of over-
      simplification, the main attitudes towards
      modernity in the muslim world.''

107. BINGER, Louis Gustave
      Esclavage, islamisme et christianisme. Paris,
      Societe d'editions scientifiques, 1891. 212p.

108. BLACHERE, R.
      ''Fes chez les geographes arabes du Moyen-age.''
      Hesparis, v.18, 1934: p.41-48.

109. BLYDEN, Edward Wilmot
Christianity, Islam and the Negro race. 2nd ed.
London, Whittingham, 1888. xv, 432p.

110. BOWERS, Aidan
''Towards an understanding of Islam.'' African
Ecclessiastical Review, v.13, No.4, 1971: p.305-314.

111. BRANDEL-SYRIER, Mia, ed.
The religious duties of Islam as taught and

explained by Abu Bakr Effendi (a translation from
the original Arabic and Afrikaans). Leiden, Brill,
1960. 198p.

112. BREMOND, (General)
L'Islam et les questions musul-manes au point de
vue francaise. Paris, Lavauzelle, 1924. 94p.

113. BRENNER, Louis
''Separate realities: a review of literature on
Sufism.'' African Historical Studies. v.5, No.4,
1972: p.637-658.

114. BROCKELMAN, C.
Geschichte der arabischen Litteratur. Weimar,
Leipder, 1898-1942. 5 vols.

115. BRUN, J.P.
''Coup d'oeil sur l'histoire des foires à travers
l'Islam.'' Recueils de la Societé Jean Bodin,
v.5, 1953: p.43-75.

116. BRUN, J.P.

''Notes sur le Tarikh el Fettach.'' Anthropos,
v.9, 1914: p.590-596.

117. CAHEN, C.

''L'hisloire economique et sociale de l'Orient
musulman medieval.'' Studia Islamica, v.3, 1955:
p.93-116.

118. CARRA DE VAUX

Les penseurs de l'Islam. Paris, Paul Geuthner,
1921.

119. CASH, William Wilson

The expansion of Islam: an Arab religion in the
non-Arab world. London, 1928.

120. CASPAR, Robert.

''L'Islam: religion et communauté.'' Cahiers des
Religions Africaines. v.4, No.7, 1970: p.97-102.
A review of a book by Louis Gardet published
in 1967 by Desclee de Brouwer.

121. CENTRE DES HAUTES ETUDES ADMINISTRATIVES SUR L'AFRIQUE
ET L'ASIE MODERNES.

Les Musulmans dans le Monde. Paris, C.H.E.A.M.
n.d.

122. CHEATA, Chafick.

La conception nouvelle de la famille musulmane
dans les recentes reformes legislatives en matiere
de mariage. Paris, Institut de Droit compare, 1966.

123. CHEATA, Chafick
''Droit musulman et droit comparé du Proche-Orient.''
Cours de Doctorat, Paris. Faculté de Droit, 1967/68.

124. ------,
Etudes de droit musulman. Paris, Presses Universi-
taires Francaises, 1971. 256p. (Travaux et Recherches.
Faculté de Droit,... Paris, serie Afrique, 7).

125. ------,
Précis de droit musulman. Paris, Dalloz, 1970.

126. CHERBONNEAU, M.A.
''Les geographes arabes au Moyen age.'' Revue de
Geographie, v.8, 1881: p.81-92.

127. COLOMER, Andre
A propos du lien entre le droit et la religion dans
les systemes juridiques orientaux: le droit musulman
existe-t-il? Paris, Institut de Droit Comparé,
1966.

128. CORBIN, Henry
Histoire de la philosophie islamique. Paris,
Gallimard, 1964. vols. (Collection idées, 38).

129. CRAGG, K.
Counsels in contemporary Islam. Edinburgh, Edinburgh University Press, 1965.

130. CUNNISON, I.
Kazembe and the Arabs to 1870. Paper presented to

130. CUNNISON, I. (Contd.)

the History of Central African Peoples Conference,
Rhodes-Livingstone Institute, Lusaka. 1963.

131. DEPONT, O. and COPPOLANI, X.
Les confreries religieuses musulmanes. Alger,
Jourdan, 1897.

132. DOI, A.R.
''The Islamic view of freedom.'' Orita. v.7, No.2,
December, 1973: p.97-112.

133. DUNLOP, D.M.
''Sources of gold and silver in Islam according
to Hamdani (10th century A.D.).'' Studia Islamica,
v.8, 1957: p.29-49.

134. FYZEE, Asaf Ali Asghar
A modern approach to Islam. Bombay, Asia Publi-
shing House, 1963. xi, 127p.

135. GARDET, Louis
La cité musulmane: vie sociale et politique. Paris,
Librairie philosophique, J. Vrin, 1954.

136. GAUDEFROY-DEMOMBYNES, Maurice
Muslim institutions. Translated from the French
by John P. MacGregor. London, Allen and Unwin,
1950. 216p.

137. GIBB, Hamilton Alexander R.
Modern trends in Islam. Chicago, University of
Chicago Press, 1950.

138. GIBB, Hamilton Alexander R.
Mohammedanism: an historical survey. 2nd ed.
London, Oxford University Press, 1953. ix, 208p.
(The Home University Library of modern knowledge,
197).

139. GOLDZIHER, Ignac
Muslim studies (Muhammedanische Studien); editêd by
S.M. Stern, translated from the German by C.R. Barber
and S.M. Stern. London, Allen & Unwin, 1967.

140. HAHN, Georges
''Bref apercu des problemes modernes de la famille
musulmane.'' Afrique et Asie, v.53, No.1, 1961:
p.20-24.

141. HAMET, Ismael
''Literature arabe saharienne.'' Revue du Monde
Musulmane, v.12, 1910: p.194-213; p.380-405.

142. HASAN, S.M.
Muslim creed and culture, an interpretation of
fundamental institutions and cultural legacies of
Islam. Dacca, Ideal Publications, 1962. 315p.

143. HILL, D.J.
''Comparative aspects of the Maliki law and common
law of agency.'' Journal, Centre for Islamic Legal
Studies (Zaria). v.1, No.2, 1967: p.53-69.

144. HOLT, Peter M. et al eds.
The Cambridge history of Islam. 2. The further
Islamic lands (including Africa and the Muslim West)

31

144. HOLT, Peter M. et al, eds. (Contd.)

Islamic society and civilization. London, Cambridge
University Press. 1970. xxvi, 966p. illus.,
Bibliography.

145. HOURANI, A.H. and STERN, S.M., eds.
The Islamic city: a coloquim. Philadelphia, University of Pennsylvania Press, 1970. 222p.

146. HUGHES, Rev. T.P.
Notes on Muhammadanism, being outlines of religious
system of Islam. 3rd ed. London, Allen, 1894.
xvi, 282p.

147. IBN BATOUTAH
Voyages. Texte arabe, accompagné d'une traduction
par C. Defremery et B.R. Sanguinetti. Paris, Imprimerie Nationale, 1922. 479p.

148. IBN BATUTA
Travels, A.D. 1325-1354; translated with revisions
and notes from the Arabic text edited by C. Defremery
and B.R. Sanguinetti, by H.A.R. Gibb. Cambridge,
Published for the Hakluyt Society at the University
Press, 1958.

149. JAMEELA, Maryam
Islam versus the West. Lahore, Ashraf, 1962. 129p.

150. KHAN, Muhammad Zafrulla
Islam: its meaning for modern man. London,
Routledge & Kegan Paul. 1962.

151.   KHOURY, A'del-Theodore

Les theologiens et l'Islam. Textes et auteurs
viiie-xiie siècle. 2e tirage. Louvain, 1969. 334p.

152.   KNAPPERT, Jan

''Utenzi wa Miiraji – the ascension of the prophet
Mohammed, by Sh. Moh. Jambein.'' Afrika und Ubersee,
v.50, No. 1/2, 1967: p.34-40.

153.   ------,

''Wilada Nabii: a praise poem on the prophet
Mohammed.'' Afrika Und Ubersee, v.50, Nos. 1/2,
1967: p.34-40.

154.   LAMMENS, Henri

Islam: beliefs and institutions. Translated from
the French by Sir E. Denison Ross. London, Frank
Cass, 1968. ix, 256p. (Islam and the Muslim world,
no.6). bibliog.

155.   The LANDS of Islam: a description of the condition of
Arabia, Afghanistam, Persia, Turkey, Morocco and
Muhamedan Negroes. Compiled from the best authorities.
London and Madras, Christian Literature Society for
India, 1897. 82p.

156.   LE TOURNEAU, Roger

''Maghribi Islam: rigourism and bewilderment.''
In Africa from early times to 1800, edited by
P.J.M. McEwan, New York, Oxford University Press,
1968: p.351-360.

157. LEVI-PROVENCAL, E.
      ''La toma de Valencia por El Cid, segun las Fuentes
      Musulmanas y el original arabe de la Cronica General
      de Espana.'' Al-Andalus, v.13, No.1, 1948: p.97-156

158. LEVY, Reuben
      The social structure of Islam. Cambridge, Cambridge
      University Press, 1962.

159. LEWIS, I.M.
      ''Islam and the modern world.'' In Africa from
      early times to 1800, edited by J.M. McEwan. New York
      Oxford University Press, 1968: p.328-342.

160. LOMBARD, M.
      ''Les bases monetaires d'une suprematie economique.
      L'or musulman du viie au xie siecle.'' Annales;
      Economies, Société, Civilisations, v.2, 1947: p.143-
      160.

161. MACCOLL, Malcolm
      ''Islam and civilization.'' The Contemporary Review
      v.53, 1888: p.537-559.

162. MACDONALD, Duncan B.
      Development of muslim theology, jurisprudence and
      constitutional theory. Beirut, Khayats, 1965. 386p.

163. MAHMUD, Kalil
      ''The concept of al-Mahdi according to the Ahmadiyya
      movement in Islam.'' Orita, v.2, No.2, December,
      1968: p.103-108.
            ''The Ahmadiyya movement... took the position
34

163. MAHMUD, Kalil (Contd.)

that the Mahdi and Jesus were one and the same
person.''

164. MAHMUD, Sayyid Fayyaz.
The story of Islam. Karachi, Dacca, Oxford
University Press, 1960. xii, 354p. illus.

165. MARTIN, B.G.
''Notes sur l'origine de la tariqa de Tiganiyya et
sur les debuts d'al-Hagg Umar.'' Revue d'Etudes
Islamiques (Paris), v.37, No.2, 1969: p.267-290.

166. MARTY, P.
''Les Fadelia.'' Revue du Monde Musulmane, v.31,
1915-16: p.135-220.

167. MAS LATRIE, M.L. de
Traites de paix et de commerce et documents divers
concernant les relations des chrétiens avec les
arabes de l'Afrique septentrionale au Moyen-Age.
Paris, Henri Plon, 1865.

168. MATHEWS, Basil Joseph
''Islam and western civilization: the influence of
western nations and western science, commerce and
thought on the Mohammedan world.'' Missionary
Review of the world, v.49, December 1926: p.937-944.

169. MAUNY, R. (and others)
Textes et documents relatifs à l'histoire des
voyages d'Ibn Battuta (1304-1377). Dakar, Université

169. MAUNY, R. (and others) (Contd.)

de Dakar. Publications de la Faculté des Lettres et Sciences Humaines (Histoire, No.9). 1966.

170. MAZAHERI, Ali

La vie quotidienne des Musulmans au Moyen-Age du Xe au XIIIe siecle. Paris, Hachette, 1951.

171. MILLIOT, Louis

''L'idée de loi dans l'Islam.'' Revue International de Droit Comparé, October-December 1952.

172. ------,

Introduction à l'étude du droit musulman. Paris, Recueil Sirey, 1953. xii, 822p. bibliog.

173. ------,

''La pensée juridique de l'Islam.'' Revue internationale de Droit Comparé, 1954.

174. ------,

Travaux de la Semaine internationale de droit Musulman, Paris, 2-7 juillet 1951. Publié avec le concours du Centre National de la Recherch Scientifique. Paris, Recueil Sirey, 1953. 161p.

175. MIQUEL, Andre

L'Islam et sa civilisation. Paris, A. Colin, 1969. 578p. illus.

176. MITCHELL, Richard Paul

The society of Muslim brothers. New York, Oxford

176.   MITCHELL, Richard Paul (Contd.)

       University Press, 1969. xix, 349p.

177.   MOLE, Marijan

       Les mystiques musulmans. Paris, Presses Universi-
       taires de France, 1965. 128p.

178.   MONTEIL, Vincent

       ''Un Coran ahmadi en Swahili.'' Bulletin de l'IFAN,
       v.29, (B) Nos. 3/4, July-October 1967: p.479-495.
       illus.

179.   ------,

       ''Ibn Khaldun, sociologue et historien.'' Revue
       Historique, April-June 1967: p.339-358.

180.   MONTGOMERY, W.

       Islamic political thought: the basic concepts.
       Edinburgh, University Press, 1968. 196p. (Islamic
       surveys, 6).

181.   MOTT, John R.

       The Moslem world today. New York, George H. Doran,
       1925. xv, 420p.

182.   al-MUQADDASI, Muhammad Ibn Ahmad

       Description de l'Orient musulman au IVe-X^e siecle.
       Texte arabe et traduction francaise par Ch. Pellat.
       Alger, Carbonel, 1950.

183.   NASSR, Seyyed Hossein

       Ideals and realities of Islam. London, Allen &
       Unwin, 1966. 184p.

184. OULD DADDAH, Abd Allah

''Ibn Bashkuwal, auteur andalou du xiie siecle, et
son dictionnaire biographique intitulé Kitab ar-Sila.
(Memoire de Diplome d'Etudes Superieures, prepared
under the supervision of Professor R. Blachere in
1961-1962).

185. PARRINDER, E.G.

''Islam.'' The Listener, v.73, No.1867, 1965:
p.17-21.

186. PEEL, W.G.

''Islam not a stepping-stone toward Christianity.''
Moslem World, October 1911: p.365-372.

187. PELLEGRIN, Arthur

L'Islam dans le monde. Nouveau ed., refondue et
mise à jour avec 4 croquis. Paris, Payot, 1950.
237p. illus. (Collection de documents et de temoig-
nages pour servir à l'histoire de notre temps).

188. PLANHOL, Xavier de

Le monde islamique: essai de geographie religieuse.
Paris, Presses Universitaires de France, 1957. 146p.
(Mythes et religions, 34).

189. PRINS, A.H.J.

''Islamic maritime magic: a ship's charm from Lamu.'
In Greschet, H.J. (and others) (eds) Wort und
religion, Stuttgart, 1969: p.294-304.

190. PROCTER, J.H. ed.

Islam and international relations. London, Pall Mal
Press, 1965.

191. PRUEN, St.

The Arab and the African. London, Seeley & Co.,
1891.

192. RAHMAN, Fazlur

Islam. New York, Holt, 1967. 271p. illus.
Introduction to and interpretation of Islamic
religion. Includes bibliography.

193. RODINSON, Maxime

Islam et capitalisme. Paris, Editions du Sevil,
1966.

194. RONDOT, Pierre

''Le Mahdisme.'' Mois en Afrique (Dakar), v.5,
May 1966: p.48-60.

195. ROSENTHAL, E.I.J.

Islam in the modern national state. Cambridge,
Cambridge University Press, 1965.

196. RUXTON, F.H.

Maliki law: a summary from French translations of
the Mukhtasar of Sidi Khalil. Published by order
of Sir F.D. Lugard. London, Luzac & Co., 1916.
xv, 420p.

197. SALLOUN, D.

The Islamic view of man. Orita, v.6, No.1, December 1962: p.87-100.

198. SAMB, Amar

''La civilisation Arabo-Musulmane: son influence

198. SAMB, Amar (Contd.)

sur le monde occidental et les causes de son declin
Notes Africaines, No.129, January 1971: p.20-28.

199. SAMB, Majhetar
La succession en droit musulman. Saint Louis,
Imprimerie du gouvernement, 1963. 96p.

200. SANNEH, Lamin
''Amulets and muslim orthodoxy.'' International
Review of Mission, v.63, No.252, October 1974:
p.515-529.

201. SCHACHT, Joseph
An introduction to Islamic law. Oxford, Clarendon
Press, 1964. viii, 304p.

202. ------,
The legacy of Islam. 2nd ed., edited by the late
Joseph Schacht with C.E. Bosworth. Oxford, Claren-
don Press, 1974. 530p. illus.
Attempts to trace some of the great unifying
lines which run through the manifestations of
Islam as a religion and a civilization. Chapter
III deals with the ''Islamic frontiers in Africa
and Asia.

203. SCHOY, S.
''The geography of the Moslems of the Middle Ages.'
Geographical Review, v.14, 1924: p.257-269.

204. SCHWERIN, Hans Hugold
      Afrika studier. Muhammedanismen i Afrika. Lund,
      Gleerup, 1892. 216p.

205. SHOEMAKER, Michael Myers
      Islam lands: Nubia, the Sudan, Tunisia and Algeria.
      New York, London, P. Putnam's sons, 1910. xii,
      251p.

206. SOURDEL, Dominique
      L'Islam. 5th ed., Paris, Presses Universitaires
      de France, 1962. 127p. (Que sais-je? Le point des
      connaissances actuelles, no.355).

207. STODDARD, Theodore L.
      The new world of Islam. New York, Charles Scribner,
      1921. vi, 362p.

208. TEFFAHI, Mourad
      Traite' de succession musulmanes d'après le rite
      malekite. Saint-Louis, Senegal, Centre IFAN
      Mauritanie, 1948. (Etudes Mauritaniennes, no.1).

209. TOUCEDA FONTENLA, R.
      ''The wearing of the pigtail among Muslims and the
      legend of its origin''/''El uso de la coleta entre
      los musulmanes y leyenda sobre el origen de la
      misma.'' Africa (Madrid), v.17, January 1960:
      p.8-10.

210. TOURE, Cheikh
      Les obligations d'un Tidjane des deux sexes. Saint-
      Louis, 1953. 29p.

211. TRIMINGHAM, John Spencer
   The sufi orders in Islam. Oxford, Clarendon Press,
   1971. ix, 333p. Bibliog.

212. TRITTON, Arthur Stanley
   Islam: belief and practices. London, Hutchinson,
   1957. viii, 200p. (Hutchinson University Library,
   World Religions Series).

213. UKNK, Khalil Ben
   Aberge de la loi musulmane selon le rite de l'Imam
   Malik. Paris, Maisonneuve, 1962.

214. WATT, William Montgomery
   The faith and practice of al-Ghazali. London,
   Allen & Unwin, 1953.

215. ------,
   Islam and the integration of society. Evanston,
   Ill., Northwestern University Press, 1961. ix,
   293p.

216. ------,
   Islamic philosophy and theology. Edinburgh,
   University Press, 1962. xxiii, 196p. (Islamic surv-
   eys, 1).

217. YAFI, Ab Dalla El
   ''La condition privée de la femme dans le droit
   de Islam.'' Thèse, Institut de Droit Comparé.
   Paris, 1925.

218. ZAMBAUR, Edward K.M. Von
     <u>Manuel de genealogie et de chronologie pour l'histoire de l'Islam</u>. Hanovre, Librairie orientaliste Heinz Lafaire, 1927.

219. ZWEMER, Samuel M.
     ''New census of the Muslim world.'' <u>Moslem World</u>, v.13, July 1923: p.282-290.

220. ------,
     <u>Mohammed or Christ: an account of the rapid spread of ·Islam in all parts of the globe... and suggested means to be adopted to counteract the evil</u>. New York, Fleming H. Revell & Co., 1915. 292p.

221. ------,
     ''The British Empire and Islam.'' <u>East and West</u>, v.22, April 1924: p.108-124.

ISLAM IN AFRICA (GENERAL)

222. ABU-LUGHOD, Ibrahim
     ''Africa and the Islamic world.'' In <u>The African experience, vol.I: essays</u>, edited by John N. Paden and Edward W. Soja. London, Heinemann Educational Books, 1970: p.545-567.

223. ADAMS, W.Y.
     ''Ethnohistory and Islamic tradition in Africa.'' <u>Ethnohistory</u>, v.16, No.4, 1969: p.277-288.

224. L'AFRIQUE Islamique. Lausanne, Theophile Grin, 1966.

225. ''L'AHMADISME en Afrique: contribution a l'étude du
     mouvement Ahmadia.'' Renseignements Coloniaux,
     v.1, 1924: p.29-36.

226. ALEXANDRE, Pierre
     ''L'Afrique noire et l'expansion de l'Islam.''
     Monde Non-Chrétien, v.36, October-December, 1955:
     p.315-334.

227. ------,
     ''Petite criteriologie pour une sociologie de
     l'Islam negro-africain.'' Afrique et Asie, v.44,
     1958: p.42-50.

228. ALLEN, Christopher and JOHNSON, R.W., eds.
     African perspectives: papers in the history,
     politics and economics of Africa presented to
     Thomas Hodgkin. Cambridge, University Press, 1970.
     xx, 439p. illus., bibliog.
         The first four papers in this book deal with
     aspects of Islam in the history of West Africa.

229. ANDERSON, James Norman Datrymple
     ''The adaptation of Muslim law in sub-Saharan
     Africa.'' African Law, 1965: p.149-164.

230. ------,
     Islamic law in Africa. With a foreword by Lord
     Hailey. London, H.M.S.O. 1954. viii, 409p.
     (Colonial Research Publication No.16).

231. ANDERSON, James N.D.
        ''Islamic law in African colonies.'' Corona,
        v.3, No.7, July 1951: p.262-266.
        Discusses the extent to which Islamic law
      is applied in Nyasaland, Uganda, Kenya and
      Tanzania, showing the variations in each state.

232. ------,
        ''Relationship between Islamic and customary law
      in Africa.'' Journal of African Administration,
      v.12, No.4, October 1960: p.228-234.
        Attempts to draw a distinction between those
      countries where Islamic law is regarded as a
      special variety of native law and custom (Northern
      Nigeria, Ghana, Sierra Leone, Uganda) and where
      it is considered as a distinct system (Somalia,
      Kenya, Zanzibar).

233. ------,
        ''Tropical Africa: infiltration and expanding
      horizons.'' In Gustav E. Von Grunebaum (ed.),
      Unity and Variety in muslim civilization.
      Chicago, University of Chicago Press, 1955.

234. ANDRÉ, F.J.
        L'Islam noir. Paris, Geuthner, 1924. 129p.

235. ATTERBURY, Anson P.
        Islam in Africa: its effects - religious, ethical,
      and social-upon the peoples of the country. New
      York, Negro Universities Press, 1969. 208p.

236. AZAM, A.P.
''Les grandes lignes de l'expansion de l'Islam
en Afrique noire.'' Document: Centre des Hautes
Etudes Administratives sur l'Afrique et l'Asie
Moderne. No.1014, 1947.

237. ------,
''L'Islam en Afrique Noire.'' Revue des Troupes
Coloniales, v.286, March 1947: p.35-47.

238. ------,
''Les limites de l'Islam africain.'' Afrique et
Asie, 1948: p.17-30.

239. BECKER, C.H.
L'Islam et la colonisation de l'Afrique; conference
faite sous le patronage de l'Union coloniale
francaise, le 22 janvier 1910. Paris, Union
Coloniale Francaise, 1910. 24p.

240. BESRASCOLI, C.
''Islam africano.'' Nigrizia, v.83, Nos. 7/8,
July/August 1965: p.14-20.

241. BLYDEN, Edward Wilmot
''The Koran in Africa.'' Journal of the African
Society, v.4, January 1905: p.157-171.

242. BONET-MAUREY, G.
L'Islamisme et le Christianisme en Afrique.
Paris, Hachette, 1906. 299p.

243. BOURNICHON, J.

L'invasion musulmane en Afrique, suivie du reveil de la foi chrétienne dans ces contrées et la croisade des noirs, entreprise par S. Em, Le Cardinal Lavigerie, archevêque d'Alger et de Carthage. 3rd ed., Tours, Cattier, 1897. 352p.

244. BRELVI, Mahmud

Islam in Africa: Foreword by M.M. Sharif. Introduction by Ishtiaq Husain Qureshi. Lahore, Institute of Islamic Culture, 1965? 657p.

A comprehensive monograph on the growth and development of Islam in Africa.

245. BRENNER, L.

''The maintenance and transmission of Islamic culture in tropical Africa.'' African Religious Research (Los Angeles) v.3, No.2, November, 1973: p.4-12.

246. BRIGGS, L.C.

Tribes of the Sahara. Cambridge, Harvard University Press, 1960. xx, 295p. illus.

247. BRUNSCHVIG, Robert

''Un texte arabe du IXe siècle interessant le Fezzan.'' Revue Africaine, v.89, 1945: p.21-25.

248. BURRIDGE, W.

''Africa, land of Mohammed.'' Ave Maria, v.94, July 1961: p.5-8.

249. CARDAIRE, Marcel

Contribution à l'étude de l'Islam noir. Douala,
Centre I.F.A.N., 1949. 120p.

250. ------,

''L'Islam et la cellule sociale africaine.''
Afrique et Asie, v.29, 1955: p.20-28.

251. CARLES, Fernand

La France et l'Islam en Afrique. Contribution à
l'étude de la politique coloniale dans l'Afrique
francaise. Toulouse, Rivière, 1915. 214p.

252. CARPENTER, George W.

''The role of Christianity and Islam in contemporary Africa.'' In Africa today, edited by C. Grove
Haines. New York, Greenwood Press, 1968: p.90-112.

253. CHAILLEY, Marcel

Notes et études sur l'Islam en Afrique noire. Paris
Peyronnet, 1962. 194p. illus. (Université de Paris,
Centre de hautes études administratives sur l'Afriq
et l'Asie modernes. Recherches et documents: serie
Afrique noire, 1).

254. COMHAIRE, J.

''Some notes on Africans in Muslim history.''
Muslim World, v.46, October 1956: p.336-344.

255. CONTEROT, E.

Relation de la nigrité contenant une exacte description des ses royaumes et de leurs gouvernements
la religion, les moeurs, coutumes et raretez de ce

255. CONTEROT, E. (Contd.)

pais. Avec la decouverte de la riviere du Senegal,
dont on a fait une carte particulière. Paris,
1968.

256. DALE, Godfrey
Islam in Africa: an introduction to the study of
Islam for African Christians. London, Society
for the Propagation of Christian Knowledge, 1925.

257. DAN FODIO, Uthman
''Islam and women.'' In Thomas Hodgkin, Nigerian
perspectives: an historical anthology. London,
Oxford University Press, 1960: p.194-195.

258. DELAFOSSE, Maurice
''L'Islam et les sociétés noires de l'Afrique.''
Bulletin du Comite d'Etudes Historiques et Scien-
tifique de l'Afrique Occidentale Francaise.
December 1922: p.321-333.

259. ------,
''Islam in Africa.'' International Review of
Missions, July 1926: p.533-568.

260. DESCHAMPS, M.
Les religions de l'Afrique Noire. Paris, Presses
Universitaires de France, 1924. 125p.

261. DIARA, Agadem L.
Islam and pan-Africanism. Detroit, Agasha Produc-
tions, 1973. 95p.

261. DIARA, Agadem L. (Contd.)

Examination of pan-Africanism in Islamic
Africa.

262. DOUTTE, E.

''L'Islam noir.'' Revue Contemporain, June
1923: p.188-196.

263. DOI, A.R.I.

''The Arab concept of Ifriqiya and the planting
of Islam in Africa.'' Africa Quarterly, v.12,
No.3, October-December 1972: p.202-214. bibliog.
A detailed and interesting account of the
planting and spread of Islam into the African
continent, with diverse interpretations of the
Arabic word ''Ifriqiya,'' meaning Africa.

264. DU PLESSIS, Johannes

''Government and Islam in Africa.'' Moslem World,
V.II, January 1921: p.1-23.

265. FADUMA, O.

''Christianity and Islam in Africa.'' Missionary
Review of the World, v.48, November 1925: p.856-
858.

266. FISHER, Humphrey J.

''Hassebu: Islamic healing in black Africa.'' In
Northern Africa: Islam and modernization, nationalism and independence, papers presented and discussed at a symposium arranged by the African
Studies Association of the United Kingdom on the

266. FISHER, Humphrey J. (Contd.)

occasion of its Annual General Meeting, 14 September 1971. Edited with an introduction by
Michael Brett. London, Cass, 1973: p.23-48.

267. ------,

Islam in Africa. New York, Van Nostrand-Reinhold,
1969.

268. ------,

''Muslim prayer and military activity in the
history of Africa south of the Sahara.'' Journal
of African History. v.12, No.3, 1971: p.391-406.

269. ------,

''The Western and Central Sudan and East Africa.''
In Holt, P.M. (ed.) The Cambridge history of
Islam, v.2, 1970: p.345-405.

270. FISHER, Allan G.B. and FISHER, Humphrey J.
Slavery and muslim society in Africa: the institu-
tion in Saharan and Sudanic Africa and the Trans-
Saharan trade. London, Hurst, 1970. 182p. bibliog.

271. FROELICH, Jean-Claude
''Islam et cultures arabe en Afrique au sud du
Sahara.'' Mois en Afrique (Dakar), v.1, 1966:
p.54-70.

272. ------,

Les musulmans d'Afrique noire. Paris, Editions
de l'Orante, 1962. 406p. illus., maps. Includes
bibliography (Lumiere et nations).

ISLAM IN AFRICA (GENERAL)

273. FROELICH, Jean-Claude
''Problemes actuels de l'Islam en Afrique noire.''
Communautés et continents, v.26, April-June, 1965:
p.35-47.

274. ------,
''Relationship between Islam in Africa north and
south of the Sahara.'' African Forum, v.3, Nos.
2/3, Fall 1967/Winter 1968: p.44-57.

275. ------,
''Sectes musulmanes èt civilizations negro-
africaines.'' Mois en Afrique, v.5, May 1966:
p.98-105.
Although Islam in Africa tolerates animism
or is prepared to accept certain deviations which
are normal among Africans, its attitude to such
sects of foreign origin as Ahmadiyya and Bahaism
is much more strict.

276. GAIRDNER, W.H.T.
''Islam in Africa: the sequel to a challenge.''
International Review of Missions, v.13, January
1924: p.3-25.

277. el-GARH, M.S.
''The philosophical basis of Islamic education in
Africa.'' West African Journal of Education, v.15
No.1, February 1971: p.8-20.

278. HAMPATE BA, Amadou
''Islam et l'Afrique noire.'' In Colloque sur les
religions, Abidjan, 5-12 Avril 1961: Paris,

52

278.   HAMPATE BA, Amadou (Contd.)

        Presence Africaine, 1962: p.101-108.

279.   HARTMANN, M.

        ''Islam and culture in Africa.'' Moslem World,
        October 1911: p.373-380.

280.   HISKETT, M.

        ''Problems of religious education in Muslim
        communities in Africa.'' Oversea Education, v.32,
        No.3, October 1960: p.117-126.

281.   HODGKIN, Thomas

        ''An Islamic scrapbook.'' Research Bulletin
        (Centre of Arabic Documentation, Ibadan University)
        1965: p.29-34.

            Review of L'Islam noir, by V. Monteil.

282.   ------,

        ''Mahdism, Messianism and Marxism in the African
        setting.'' In Hasan, Y.F. ed. Sudan in Africa,
        Khartoum, 1971: p.109-127.

283.   HOLWAY, James D.

        ''Christianity and Islam in Africa-looking ahead.''
        Missionalia, v.2, No.1, 1974: p.3-17, p.262-273.

284.   ''The IMPACT of Islam in Africa.'' In The African
        experience, vol.II, syllabus; edited by John N.
        Paden and Edward W. Soja. London, Heinemann
        Educational Books, 1970: p.81-84.

285. ''ISLAM: Africa's booming faith.'' Look, v.25,
     March 1961: p.38-39.

286. ''ISLAM and African music.'' In Essays on music and
     history in Africa, edited by K.P. Wachsmann.
     Evanston, Ill., Northwestern University Press,
     1971: p.143-184.

287. ''ISLAM in Africa.'' Contributors: J. Spencer,
     Trimingham and others. Edited by James Kritzech
     and William H. Lewis. New York, 1969. viii,
     339p. illus.

288. ''ISLAM in Africa.'' In African systems of thought,
     edited by M. Fortes and G. Dieterlen. London,
     Oxford University Press, 1965: p.28-30.

289. L'ISLAM noir: contribution a l'étude des confreries
     religieuses islamiques en Afrique occidentale
     suivie d'une étude sur l'Islam au Dahomey. Paris,
     Geuthner, 1924. 131p.

290. ''ISLAM und Afrikaforschung.'' Aus Allen weltteilen,
     v.14, 1833: p.289-292.

291. ''ISLAMIC reformation movements.'' In The African
     experience, vol.2, the syllabus, by John N. Paden
     and Edward W. Soja. Evanston, Northwestern
     University Press, 1970: p.201-203.
        Short account of Islam as an agent of social
     change in Africa.

ISLAM IN AFRICA (GENERAL)

292. JALABERT, Louis
''La fermentation de l'islam noir.'' Etudes
(Paris), May 20, 1925: p.448-455.

293. JEFFREYS, M.D.W.
''Arab influence on Africa; Arab's knowledge of
the Niger.'' The Islamic Review, March 1956:
p.33-34.

294. KETTELER, R.A.
''Afrika und die Bewegung des Islam.'' (Review of
Islam noire, by V. Monteil). Neues Afrika, v.6,
No.6, June 1964: p.199-201.

295. KHANE, Amadou
''Les confreries dans l'Islam africain.'' Afrique
en marche, No.1, January 1957: p.3-5, No.2, February: p.3-5, No.3, April: p.3-5.

296. ------,
''Religions et traditions d'Afrique noire, survi-
vances animistes en pays musulmans.'' Afrique
en Marche, No.5, June-July, 1957: p.3-5, No.6,
July-August, 1957: p.3-5, Nos. 7/8, August-October
1957: p.3-8.

297. KRITZECK, James and LEWIS, William H. (eds.)
Islam in Africa. New York, Van Nostrand: London,
Reinhold, 1969. 339p.

298. LABOUNE, R.
''L'Islam et les troupes noire.'' Revue de Paris,
April 1923: p.575-602.

55

299. LE GRIP, A.
''Le Mahdisme en Afrique noire.'' L'Afrique et l'Asie, No.18, 1952: p.3-16.

300. LEVTZION, N.
''Oral traditions and Arabic documents in the Muslim historiography of Africa.'' Paper read at the Second International Congress of Africanists Dakar, 1967.

301. LEWICKI, T.
''L'Afrique noire dans le Kitab al-Masalik wal'l Mamalik d'Abu 'Ubayd al-Bakri, xi^e siecle.'' Africana Bulletin, No.2, 1965: p.9-14.

302. ------,
''Les ecrivains arabes du Moyen-Age au sujet des mines de pierres precieuses et de pierre fines en territoire africain et de leur exploitation.'' Africana Bulletin, v.7, 1967: p.49-68.

303. McKAY, Vernon
''Islam and relations among the new African states In Islam and international relations, edited by J.H. Proctor, New York, Praeger, 1964: p.164-166.

304. MALLA, Claude F.
''Some aspects of Islam in Africa south of the Sahara.'' International Review of Missions, v.56, No.224, October 1967: p.459-468.

305. MARAIS, Ben
''Islam: political factor in Africa.'' Bulletin
of the African Institute of South Africa, March
1971: p.51-64.
Surveys Islam as a political factor in Africa
in the context of Soviet-African relations.

306. MASSINGNON, Louis
''Causes et modes de la propagation de l'Islam
parmi les populations paiennes de l'Afrique.''
Rome, Atti dell'VIII Convegno, Reale Academia d'
Italia (1940): p.5-12.

307. MAZRUI, Ali A.
''Islam and the English language in East and West
Africa.'' In Whiteley, W.H. (ed.) Language use
and social change, 1971: p.179-197.

308. ------,
''Islam, political leadership and economic radi-
calism in Africa.'' Comparative Studies in
Society and History, v.9, No.3, April 1967:
p.274-291.

309. MERENSKY, Alexander
Mohammedanismus und christenthum in Kampfe um die
negerlander Afrikas. Berlin, Berliner evangelis-
che missionsgessellschaft, 1893. 20p.

310. MILLER, W.R.S.
''Islam in Africa.'' International Review of
Missions, July 1926: p.533-568.

311.   MOLLA, Claude F.
       ''Some aspects of Islam in Africa south of the
       Sahara.'' International Review of Missions, v.56,
       No.224, October 1967: p.459-468.
       ''Sociologically, Islam emerges as an African
       reality in animist eyes, identified as a society
       with partriarchal structures, an open community;
       a ladder for moving upwards in society, a form
       of patriotism, and a means of entry into the world
       of traders.''

312.   MONTEIL, Vincent
       ''Al-Bakri (Cordoue 1068), routier de l'Afrique
       blanche et noire du Nord-Ouest. Traduction
       nouvelle de seize chapitres, avec notes et commen-
       taire (sur le manuscrit arabe 17 Bd—PSS/902 du
       British Museum).'' Bulletin de l'Institut Fonda-
       mental d'Afrique Noire, v.30, serie B, No.1, 1968:
       p.39-116. illus.

313.   ------,
       ''Contribution à l'étude de l'Islam en Afrique
       noire.'' In Colloque sur les religions, Abidjan,
       5-12 Avril, 1961. Paris, Présence Africaine,
       1962: p.119-132.

314.   ------,
       L'Islam noir. 2nd ed. Paris. Edition du Seuil,
       1971: 415p. illus. Bibliog. Also in Revue Tunisien
       de Sciences Sociales (Tunis), v.2, No.4, December
       1965: p.31-54.

315.   MONTEIL, Vincent
       ''O. Islao na Africa negra.'' Afro-Asia
       (Salvador, Brazil), No. 4/5, 1967: p.5-22.

316.   ------,
       ''Sur l'arabisation des langues negro-africaines.''
       Geneve-Afrique, v.2, No.1, 1963: p.12-20.

317.   MUBARAK, Ahamad Mirza
       Islam in Africa. Rabwah, Pakistan, Ahmadiyya
       Muslim Foreign Missions Office, 1962. 41p.

318.   NDIAYE, Aissatou
       ''Sur la transcription des vocables africains
       par Ibn Bathutah.'' Notes Africaines, v.38,
       1948: p.26-27. v.41, 1949: p.31.

319.   N'GOMA, A.
       ''L'Islam noir.'' Presence Africain, Nos.8/9,
       1950: p.333-343.
            A brief historical sketch of the spread of
       Islam into Tropical Africa.

320.   ONIBONOJE, G.O.
       Africa from the rise of Islam to the end of
       slave trade. Ibadan, Onibon-Oje Press, 1965.

321.   PANIKKAR, K.M.
       The Serpent and the Crescent; a history of the
       negro empires of Western Africa. New York,
       Asia Publishing House, 1963.

322. PEHAUT, Yves

    ''L'ouest africain au Moyen Age.'' Cahiers d'
Outre-Mer. v.60, 1962: p.407-414.

323. PHILBERT

    La conquete pacifique de l'interieur africain:
Negres, Musulmans, et Chrétiens. Paris, Lerous,
1889. 382p.

324. POGSON, T.W.

    ''Islam sweeps into the new Africa.'' Saturday
Night, v.76, October 1961: p.9-11.

325. ''RELIGION today. 6. Islam in Africa.'' Hibbert
Journal, v.61, January 1963: p.57-60.

326. RICHARD-MOLARD, Jacques

    L'Islam comme ferment cyclique en Afrique noire.
Document. Centre des Hautes Etudes Administratives
sur l'Afrique et l'Asie Modernes, No.1682. 1950.

327. SCHIEFFELIN, Henry Maunsell

    The people of Africa: a series of papers on their
character, condition and future prospects, by
E.W. Blyden (and others).

    Chapter II is on the 'Koran and African
Mohammedanism' contributed by Tayler Lewis.

328. SCHULTZE, Arnold

    The Sultanate of Bornu. Translated by P.A.
Benton. London, Frank Cass, 1968 (Cass Library
of African Studies: General Studies, no.50).

329. SELL, E.
''Islam in Africa.'' Moslem World, v.1, 1911:
p.136-146.

330. SHEPPARD, Roscoe Burton
Islamic Africa. New York, Cincinati, Methodist
Book Concern, 1914. 127p.

331. SCIOU, Chef de bataillon
La religion musulmane et ses caractères particu-
liers en Afrique noir francaise. Document,
Centre Militaire d'Information et Specialisation
pour l'Outremer. 1957.

332. ''SPREAD and influence of Islam.'' In Africa from
early times to 1800, edited by P.J.M. McEwan.
New York, Oxford University Press, 1968: p.328-367.
Contents: ''Islam and the modern world,'' by
I.M. Lewis; ''Islam in East Africa,'' by J. Spencer
Trimingham; ''Maghribi Islam: Rigourism and
Bewilderment,'' by Roger le Tourneau; ''Islam and
National Movements in West Africa,'' by Thomas
Hodgkin.

333. SURET-CANALE, Jean
Afrique noire, occidentale et centrale, geographie,
civilization, histoire. Preface de Jean Dresch.
2 ed. revue et mise a jour. Paris, Editions
Sociale, 1961. 321p.

334. TESCAROLI, Cirillo
''Islam africano.'' Nigrizia (Verona) v.83, Nos.
7/8, July-August 1965: p.14-20. illus.

ISLAM IN AFRICA (GENERAL)

335. THOMAS, Louis-Vincent
''L'Africain et le sacré (reflexions sur le
devenir des religions).'' Bulletin de l'Institut
Fondamental d'Afrique Noire, v.29, Serie B, No.3/4
1967: p.619-677.

336. TRIMINGHAM, John Spencer
The influence of Islam upon Africa. Harlow,
Longmans, 1968. x, 159p. (Arab background series).

337. ------,
''.The phases of Islamic expansion and Islamic
culture zones in Africa.'' In Islam in Tropical
Africa, edited by I.M. Lewis. London, Oxford
University Press, 1966: p.127-143.

338. ''The UNITY of God and the community of mankind:
cooperation between African muslims and African
Christians in work and witness.'' Study Encounter
v.11, No.1, 1975.
Text of a memorandum agreed upon by the
participants of regional Muslim-Christian dialogue
held in Legon, University of Ghana, July 1974.

339. VILHENA, E. Jaaquin
''Influencia islamica na costa oriental d'Africana
Boletim, Sociedade de Geografia de Lisboa, v.24,
No.5, No.7, p.197-218.

340. WALLIS, C.B.
''The influence of Islam on African native law.''
Moslem World, v.11, 1921: p.145-168.

341. WALLIS, John R.

''The historiography of Islam in Africa: the last decade (1960-1970).'' African Studies Review, (East Lansing) v.14, No.3, December 1971: p.403-424. bibliog.

342. WORDSWORTH, J.

''Islam and Christianity in Africa.'' Missionary Review of the World, v.32, September 1909: p.691-695.

343. ZWEMER, S.M.

''Islam in Africa.'' Moslem World, July 1925: p.217-222. International Review of Missions, July 1926: p.533-568.

344. ------,

''Islam in Africa today.'' Mededeelingen Tijdschrift voor Zendingswetenschap. 1927: p.116-123.

WESTERN SUDAN (GENERAL)

345. AL-HAJJ, Muhammad A.

''Hayatu B. Sa'id: a revolutionary Mahdist in the Western Sudan.'' In Hasan, Y.F. ed. Sudan in Africa, Khartoum, 1971: p.128-141.

346. AWE, Balanle

''Empires of the Western Sudan: Ghana, Mali, Songhai.'' In Thousand years of West African

346. AWE, Balanle (Contd.)

history, edited by J.F.A. Ajayi and I. Espie.
Camden, N.J. Nelson, 1967: p.55-71.

347. BARGES, Abbe J.J.L.
''Memoire sur les relations commerciales de
Tlemencen avec le Soudan sous le regne des Beni
Zeyan.'' Revue de l'Orient de l'Algerie et des
colonies (1853): p.337-348.

348. BESLAY, Capt.
''Apercu sur les croyances, coutumes, et institu-
tions des Maures.'' Memoires. Centre des Hautes
Etudes d'Administration Musulmane No.1415, n.d.

349. BLYDEN, Edward Wilmot
''Islam in Western Sudan.'' Journal of the
African Society, v.2, 1902: p.11-37.

350. BOISNARD, Magali
Sultans de Touggourt. Histoire d'une dynastie et
d'un royaume sahariens, d'après le folklore et
les documents contemporains. Paris, Geuthner,
1933.

351. BOVILL, E.W.
Caravans of the old Sahara; an introduction to the
history of the Western Sudan. Oxford University
Press, 1968.

352. ------,
The golden trade of the Moors. 2nd ed. revised

352. BOVILL, E.W. (Contd.)

> and with additional material by Robin Hallett.
> London, Oxford University Press, 1968.

353. ------,

> ''The Moorish invasion of the Sudan.'' Journal
> of the African Society, v.26, 1926: p.245-262.
> p.380-387, v.27, 1927: p.47-56.

354. ------,

> ''Saharan explorers of the fifteenth century.''
> Journal of the African Society. V.28, 1928/29:
> p.19-37.

355. BRETT, M.

> ''Ifriqiya as a market for Saharan trade from
> the tenth to the twelfth century A.D.'' Journal
> of African History, v.10, 1969: p.347-364.

356. CAILLIE, Rene

> Journal d'un voyage à Temboctou et à Jenne, dans
> l'Afrique centrale, precedé d'observations faites
> chez les Maures, Braknas, les Nalous et d'autres
> peuples. Paris, 1830. 3 vols.

357. ------,

> Travels through Central Africa to Timbuctoo.
> London, Henry Colburn and Richard Bentley. 1830.
> 2 vols.

358. el-CHENNAFI, M.

> ''Sur les traces d'Awdaghust: les Tagdawest et

358. el-CHENNAFI, M. (Contd.)

les ancienne cite.'' In Robert, D.S. and Devisse,
J. Tegdaoust I: recherches sur Aoudaghost. Paris,
1970: p.97-107.

359. CORNEVIN, Robert
''Voyages musulmans aux Canaries du XIIIe siècle.''
Notes Africaines. No.96, 1962. 128p.

360. CROWTHER, Samuel Adjai
Experience with the heathens and Mohamedans in
West Africa. London, Society for Promoting
Christian Knowledge, 1892. 60p.

361. CHERBONNEAU, M.A.
''Essai sur le litterature arabe au Soudan d'après
le Tekmilet et Dibadj d'Ahmed Baba le Tombouctien.''
Annuaire de Sociologie et Archeologie Constantine,
v.2, 1854-1855: p.1-42.

362. DAVEAU, S.
''Itineraire de Tamadalt à Awdaghust selon al-Bakri
In Robert D.S. and Devisse, J. Tegdaoust I:
recherches sur Aoudaghost. Paris, 1970: p.33-38.

363. DAVIDSON, Basil
''Kingdoms of the Old Sudan.'' In Black history,
edited with commentary by M. Drimmer, New York,
Doubleday, 1968.

364. DELAFOSSE, Maurice
''Les noms de musulmans de Soudan occidental.''
Revue du Monde Musulman, v.12, 1910: p.257-261.

365. DELAFOSSE, M.

Notes sur les manuscrits acquis en 1911 et 1912
par M. Bonnel de Mezieres dans la region de
Tombouctou-Oualata (Haut-Senegal et Niger).
Annales et Memoire de CAOF. 1916: p.120-129.

366. ------,

''Les relations du Maroc avec le Soudan à travers
les ages.'' Hesperis (Rabat), v.4, 1924: p.153-
174.

367. ------,

''Traditions historiques et legendaires du Soudan
occidental,'' traduits d'un manuscrit arabe.
Bulletin du Comité de l'Afrique Francaise: Rensei-
gnement coloniaux. 1913: p.293-306; 325-329,
355-368.

368. DEVISSE, J.

''La question d'Audaghust.'' In Robert, D.S. and
Devisse, J. Tegdaoust I: recherches sur Aoudaghost.
Paris, 1970: p.109-156.

369. DIAKILE, Mamadou Aissa Kaba

''Livre renfermant la genealogie des diverses
tribus noires du Soudan et l'histoire des rois
après Mohamet, suivant les renseignements fournis
par certaines personnes et ceux recueillis dans
les anciens livres.'' Avant-propos de H. Labouret.
Annales de l'Academie des Sciences Coloniales,
v.3, 1929: p.189-225.

370. GADEN, H.

''Les Salines d'Aoulil.'' Revue du Monde Musulman,
v.12, No.11, November 1910: p.436-443.

371. GALAND, L.

''Les noms d'Awdagast et de Tagdawst.'' In
Robert, D.S. and Devisse, J. Tegdaoust I:
recherches sur Aoudaghost. Paris, 1970: p.29-30.

372. GERBEAU, H.

''La region de l'Issa-Ber. Ancienne route d'
invasions, zone marginale des grands empires
soudanais, trait d'union entre le Macina et
Tombouctou.'' Etudes d'Outre-Mer (1959): p.51-58,
91-108.

373. HAMMONI, Mohamed Lamine Ould

''Les confreries religieuse dans la société maure.'
Memoire de l'Ecole Nationale de la France Outre-
Mer, 1958-59.

374. HASAN, Yusuf Jadl

The Arabs and the Sudan: from the seventeenth to
the early sixteenth century. Edinburgh, Edinburgh
University Press, Chicago, Aldine Press, 1967.

375. HODGKIN, Thomas

''Kingdoms of the Western Sudan.'' In The dawn
of African history, edited by Roland Oliver.
London, Oxford University Press, 1961: p.37-44.

376. IBN RAHHAL, Muhammad

''Le Soudan au XVIe siècle, traduit de l'original

376. IBN RAHHAL, Muhammad (Contd.)

   arabe par M'Hammed ben Rahhal.'' Bulletin de
   la Société de Geographie et d'Archeologie de la
   Province d'Oran, v.7, 1887: p.320-331.

377. KOWALSKA, M.

   ''Zwei wenig bekannte muslimische Reisende in
   West-Sudan im 13.'' Jahrundert. Folia orientalia,
   v.3, Nos. 1/2 1961: p.231-242.

378. LA CHAPELLE, F. de.

   ''Esquisse d'une histoire du Sahara occidental.''
   Hesperis, v.11, 1930: p.35-95.

379. LAW, R.C.C.

   ''Garamantes and trans-Saharan enterprise in
   classical times.'' Journal of African History,
   v.8, No.2, 1967: p.181-200.

380. LEMOYNE, Robert

   ''Penetration des Maures en Afrique noire.''
   Memoire de Centre des Hautes Etudes d'Administration Musulmane, No.1009, 1946.

381. LESSARD, J.M.

   ''Sijilmassa - la ville et ses relations commerciales au xi[e] siecle d'apres El-Bekri.''
   Hesperis-Tamuda, v.11, 1970: p.5-36.

382. LEVTZION, N.

   ''Ibn Hawqal, the check and Awdaghost.'' Journal
   of African History, v.9, No.2, 1968: p.223-233.

383.   LEVTZION, N.
       ''The long march of Islam in the Western Sudan.''
       In R. Oliver (ed). The middle age of African
       history. London, Oxford University Press, 1967:
       p.13-18.

384.   ------,
       ''Patterns of Islamization in the Western Sudan.''
       In Oliver, R. (ed). The middle age of African
       history. London 1967: p.13-18.

385.   LEWICKI, T.
       ''A propos du nom de l'oasis de Koufra chez les
       geographes arabes du xie et du xiie siècle.''
       Journal of African History, v.6, No.3, 1965:
       p.295-306.

386.   ------,
       ''L'état nord-africain de Tahert et ses relations
       avec le Soudan occidental à la fin du viiie et au
       ixe siècle.'' Cahiers d'Etudes Africaines, v.2,
       1962: p.513-535.

387.   ------,
       ''Quelques extraits inedits relatifs aux voyages
       des commercants et des missionaires Ibadites
       nord-africains au pays du Soudan occidental au
       moyen age.'' Folia Orientalia. (Cracovie), v.2,
       1960: p.1-27.

388.   ------,
       ''Pages d'histoire du commerce trans-Saharien:

388. LEWICKI, T. (Contd.)

les commercants et les missionaires Ibadits au
Soudan central et occidental aux viiie-xii^e
siècles.'' Pzeglad Orientalistyczny, v.3, 1961:
p.3-18.

389. ------,

''Survivance chez les Berberes medievaux d'ere
musulmane de cultes anciens et de croyances
paiennes.'' Folia Orientalia, v.8, 1966: p.5-40.

390. ------,

''Traits d'histoire du commerce transsaharien:
marchands et missionnaires ibadites au Soudan
occidental et central au cours des viiie-xx^e
siècles.'' Ethnographia Polska, v.8, 1964:
p.291-311.

391. LHOTE, Henri

''Contribution à l'étude des Touareg soudanais.
Les Saghmara, les Maghcharen, les expeditions de
l'Askia Mohammed en Air et la confusion Tadekka-
Tademekka.'' Bulletin de l'Institut Fondamental
d'Afrique Noire, series B, v.17, 1955: p.334-370.

392. ------,

''Contributinn a l'histoire des Touareg soudanais.
Les limites de l'empire de Mali, la route de Gao
à l'Air et au Caire, les Tademekket dans la
region de Tombouctou, les Songai dans l'Adrar
des Iforas.'' Bulletin de l'Institut Fondamental
d'Afrique Noire, series B, v.18, 1956: p.391-407.

393.   LIGHTON, G.
          ''Islam in the Western and Central Sudan.''
          The Moslem World, v.26, No.3, July 1936: p.253-
          273.

394.   McCALL, Daniel F.
          ''The Maghrib and the Sudan: their relations in
          the past.'' Africa Forum, v.3, 1967: p.75-81.

395.   MALOWIST, M.
          ''The social and economic stability of the
          Western Sudan in the Middle Ages.'' Past and
          Present, v.33, No.3, 1966: p.3-15.

396.   MARTY, Paul
          Etudes sur l'Islam et les tribus du Soudan.
          Paris, E. Leroux, 1920-21. 4 vols.
          Vol.1 : Les Kounta de l'Est, les Berabich, les
                  Iguellad.
          Vol.2 : La region de Tombouctou, Dienne, le
                  Macina et dependances.
          Vol.3 : Les tribus Maures du Sahel et du Hodh.
          Vol.4 : La region de Kayes, le pays Bambara, le
                  Sahel de Nioro.

397.   ------,
          Etudes sur l'Islam et les tribus maures (1) Les
          Brakna. Paris, E. Leroux, 1921. 204p.

398.   ------,
          Etudes sur l'Islam maure: Cheikh Sidia, les
          Fadelia, les Ida ou Ali. Paris, E. Leroux, 1916.

399. MAUNY, Raymond
''Une route prehistorique à travers le Sahara occidentale.'' Bulletin de l'Institut Fondamental d'Afrique Noire. V.9, 1947: p.341-357.

400. MIRANDA, A.H.
''Un nuevo Manuscrito de Al-Bayan al-mughrib.'' Al-Andalus, v.24, No.1, 1959: p.63-84.

401. MISKE, Ahmad
''Une tribu maraboutique du Sahel: Les Ahel Barikalla.'' Bulletin du Comité d'Etudes Historiques et Scientifique de l'Afrique Occidentale française, v.20, 1937: p.482-506.

402. MONOD, Theodore
''Sur les inscriptions arabes peintes de Timmissao, Sahara central.'' Journal de la Société des Africanistes (1938): p.83-95.

403. NEWBURY, C.W.
''North African and Western Sudan trade in the nineteenth-century: a re-evaluation.'' Journal of African History, v.7, No.2, 1966: p.233-246.

404. NORRIS, H.T.
''Yemenis in the Western Sahara.'' Journal of African History, v.3, No.2, 1962: p.317-322.

405. PALMER, Herbert Richmond
''The Central Sahara and Sudan in the XIIth century A.D.'' Journal of the African Society, 1928-29: p.368-

406.   PALMER, Sir Herbert Richmond
           ''The Kingdom of Gaoga of Leo Africanus.''
           Journal of the African Society, v.29, 1929/1930:
           p.280-284; 350-369.

407.   ------,
           Sudanese memoirs; being mainly translations of a
           number of Arabic manuscripts relating to the
           Central and Western Sudan. London, Cass, 1967.
           3v. (Cass library of African Studies - Central
           Studies, no.4).

408.   ------,
           ''Western Sudan history being the Raudatu l-Afkari
           Journal of the African Society, v.15, No.59, 1915-
           1916: p.261-273.

409.   PERES, H.
           ''Relation entre le Tafilelt et le Soudan à
           travers les Sahara, du xiie au xive siècles.''
           In Melanges de geographie et d'orientalisme
           offerts à'F.F. Gautier. Tours, 1937: p.409-414.

10.   ROBERT, D.S.
           Les fouilles de Tegdaoust.''   Journal of African
           History. V.11, 1970: p.471-493.

1.   ROBERT, D.S. and DEVISSE, J.
           Tegdaoust I: recherches sur Aoudaghost. Paris,
           Arts et metiers graphiques, 1970. 2 vols.

      ROOME, W.J.W.
           ''Islam in the Western and Eastern Sudan.''
           Moslem World, April 1914: p.120-136.

413. SCHACHT, Joseph
''Sur la diffusion des formes d'architecture
religieuse musulmane à travers le Sahara.''
Travaux de l'Institut de Recherches Sahariennes,
v.11, 1954: p.11-27, 1958: p.221-222.

414. SEIDEL, H.
''Islam und moscheen in westlichen Sudan.''
Globus, v.61, No.21, 1892: p.328-331.

415. SILLA, O.
''Villes historiques de l'Afrique Saharo-Soudanaise.
Revue Francaise d'Etudes Politiques Africaines,
No.29, 1968: p.25-37.

416. STEPNIEWSKA, Barbara.
''Portée sociale de l'Islam au Soudan occidentale,
aux XIVe-XVIe siecles.'' Africana Bulletin
(Warsaw), v.14, 1971: p.35-58.

417. ------,
''La propagation de l'Islam au Soudain occidental
entre le XIIe et XVIe siecles.'' These de doctorat
Faculté d'Histoire de l'Université de Varsovie,
1970. Compte-rendu in Africana Bulletin, v.13,
1970: p.112-114.

418. TRIAUD, Jean-Louis
Islam et sociétés Soudanaises au moyen-âge: étude
historique. Paris, Centre Nationale de la Recherche Scientifique, 1973. 236p. bibliog. (Recherche
Voltaique, no.16).

418. TRIAUD, Jean-Louis (Contd.)

This work is a compendium of sources on medieval African Islam. It interpretes the spread of Islam in Africa from the commercial view point.

419. VIRE, M.M.

''Stêle funeraires musulmanes soudano-sahariennes. Bulletin de l'IFAN, v.21, 1959: p.459-500.

420. WESTERMANN, D.

''L'Islam au Soudan occidental et central.'' Foi et Vie (1913): p.433-440; 494-501; 553-559.

421. ------,

''Islam in the West and Central Sudan.'' International Review of Missions, October 1912: p.618-653.

422. WILKS, Ivor

''The transmission of Islamic learning in the Western Sudan.'' In Goody, J.R. ed. Literacy in traditional societies. Cambridge, Cambridge University Press, 1968: p.161-197.

23. WILLIS, C.A.

''Religious confraternities of the Soudan.'' Soudan notes and Records, v.4, 1921: p.175-194.

24. WILLIS, John Ralph

''The Western Sudan from the Moroccan invasion to the death of Mukhtar al-Kunti (1811).'' In

424. WILLIS, John Ralph (Contd.)

J. Ajayi and M. Crowder, (eds.) History of West Africa, v.1, 1971: p.441-483.

425. ZOGHBY, Samir M.
''The impact of the Western Sudanic empires on the trans-Saharan trade, tenth to sixteenth century.'' Unpublished Ph.D. dissertation, Department of History, Georgetown University, 1966.

THE ALMORAVIDS AND THE ALMOHADS

426. AMILHAT, P.
''Les Almoravides au Sahara.'' Revue Militaire de l'Afrique Occidentale Francaise, 15, July 1937: p.1-3.

427. ------,
''Petite chronique des Ida ou Aich, heritiers guerriers des Almoravides sahariens.'' Revue des Etudes Islamiques, v.11, 1937: p.41-120.

428. BERAUD-VILLARS, Jean
Les Touareg au pays du Cid: les invasions almoravides en Espagne aux xie et xiie siècles. Avec 8 gravures hors texte, 8 croquis dans le texte et une carte. Paris, Plon, 1946: 295p. illus.

429. BOSCH-VILA, J.

Los Almoravides. Tetuan: Instituto General
Franco de estudios y investigactiones hispano-
arabes, 1956.

430. DE MORAES FARIAS, Paulo F.

‘‘The Almoravids: some questions concerning the
character of the movement during its periods of
closest contact with the Western Sudan.’’
Bulletin de l'Institut Fondamental d'Afrique
Noire, v.29, (B) Nos 3/4, July-October 1967:
p.794-874. illus., bibliog.

431. FENDALL, L. W.

‘‘The Almoravid ribat.’’ (seminar paper)
Institute of African Studies, University of
Ghana, 1965. (mimeographed)

432. LEVTZION, Nehemia

‘‘Abd Allah Ibn Yasin and the Almoravids.’’ In
J.R. Willis, (ed). Studies in West African
Islamic history: I, the cultivators of Islam.
London (forthcoming)

433. MIRANDA, A.H.

‘‘El-Rawd al-Qirtas y los Almoravides-Estudio
critico.’’ Hesperis-Tamuda, v.1, No.3, 1960:
p.515-541.

434. ------,

‘‘Nuevas aportaciones de Al-Bayan Al-Mughrib
sobre los Almoravides.’’ Al-Andalus, v.28, No.2,
1963: p.313-330.

435. MIRANDA, A.H.
      ''La Salida de los Almoravides del Desierto y el
      Reinado de Yusuf b. Tashfin.'' Hesperis, Nos.3/4,
      1959: p.155-182.

436. NORRIS, H.T.
      ''New evidence on the life of Abdullah b. Yasin
      and the origins of the Almoravid movement.''
      Journal of African History, v.12, 1971: p.260-262.

437. SEMONIN, P.
      ''The Almoravid movement in the western Sudan:
      a review of the evidence.'' Transactions of the
      Historical Society of Ghana, v.7, 1964: p.42-59.
      map.

438. TERRASSE, H.
      ''Le role des Almoravides dans l'histoire de l'
      occident.'' In Melanges Louis Halphen, Paris,
      1951.

439. WATT, William Montgomery
      ''The decline of the Almohads: reflections on the
      viability of religious movements.'' History of
      Religions, v.4, No.1, 1964: p.23-29.

440. al-ZARQASHI, Muhammad Ibn Ibrahim
      Chroniques des Almohades et des Hafcides attribuée
      à Zerkechi. Traduit par Fagnan. Constantine,
      Imprimerie Adolphe Braham, 1895.

441. ALEXANDRE, Pierre
''A West African Islamic movement: Hamallism in
French West Africa.'' In Rotberg, R.I. and
Mazrui, Ali A. Protest and power in black Africa.
New York, Oxford University Press, 1970: p.497-512
    Describes the origins of the Tijani order,
its historical background, development of
Hamallism, its effect on the French administra-
tion in West Africa, and evaluates the failures
and achievements of the Hamallist movement.

442. ANDRÉ, Pierre J.
L'Islam noir; contribution à l'étude des confrerie
religieuses islamiques en Afrique occidentale,
suivi d'une étude sur l'Islam au Dahomey. Paris,
Geuthner 1924. xx, 131p.

443. BLYDEN, Edward W.
''Islam in West Africa.'' Latitude, v.1, No.2,
1961: p.5-12.

444. BRAVMAN, Rene A.
Islam and tribal art in West Africa. Cambridge,
Cambridge University Press, 1974. 190p. (African
Studies Series).
    ''The author is an art historian who uses a
detailed study of representational art associated
with shrines and with masked cults to disprove
many of the assumptions about Islam's destructive
effects that have been passed from scholar to
scholar unchallenged and unproved.''

445. BUSSON, H.

''L'Islam dans l'Afrique occidentale d'après
l'ouvrage de Le Chatelier.'' Annales de Géogra-
phie, No.45, 1900.

446. DELAFOSSE, Maurice

''L'ahmadisme et son action en Afrique occidentale
francaise.'' Bulletin du Comité d'Etudes Historique et Scientifique de l'Afrique Occidentale
Francaise, January 1924: p.32-37.

447. ------,

''L'animisme negre et sa resistance a l'Islamisation en Afrique occidentale.'' Revue du Monde
Musulmane, March 1922: p.121-162.

448. DOI, A.R.I.

''Political role of Islam in West Africa.''
Africa Quarterly, v.7, No.4, January-March 1968:
p.335-341.

449. ELLIS, George W.

''Islam as a factor in West African culture.''
Journal of Race Development, v.2, No.2, October
1911: p.105-130.

450. FAURE, Adolphe

''Islam in North-West Africa (Maghrib). In
Religion in the Middle East, vol.2, edited by
A.J. Arberry. New York, Cambridge University
Press, 1969.

451. FISHER, Humphrey J.
      Ahmadiyyah; a study in contemporary Islam on the
      West African coast. London, Published for the
      Nigerian Institute of Social and Economic Research
      by Oxford University Press, 1963. 206p. bibliog.
          A study in four parts. Pt.I describes Islam
      in West Africa. Pt.II discussed the Islamic
      doctrine and Pts.III and IV give an account of
      the Islamic movement with emphasis on educational
      efforts.

452. ------,
      ''Muslim and Christian separatism in Africa.''
      In W.M. Watt. Religion in Africa. Edinburgh,
      University Centre of African Studies, 1964:
      p.9-23.
          A comparative study of Islamic and Christian
      separatist movements in West Africa.

453. ------,
      ''Some reflexions on Islam in independent West
      Africa.'' Clergy Review, v.53, No.3, March
      1968: p.178-190.

454. FROELICH, Jean-Claude
      ''Essai sur les causes et methodes de l'Islamisa-
      tion de l'Afrique de l'Ouest du xie siècle au xx^e
      siècle.'' In Islam in Tropical Africa, edited
      by I.M. Lewis. London, Oxford University Press,
      1966: p.160-173.

455. GOODY, Jack
      ''The impact of Islamic writing on the oral
      cultures of West Africa.'' Cahiers d'Etudes
      Africaines (Paris), v.11, No.3, 1971: p.455-466.
      Bibliog.

456. GOUILLY, A.
      ''L'Islam en Afrique occidentale.'' Monde
      Francaise, v.26, No.49, October 1949: p.35-52;
      No.50, November 1949: p.258-284.

457. ------,
      L'Islam dans l'Afrique occidentale francaise.
      Paris, Larose, 1952. 318p. illus.
          A scholarly study of Islam in French Africa.
      Traces the history of Islamic conquests from the
      11th century to the period of French control.

458. HODGKIN, Thomas
      ''The fact of African history: Islam in West
      Africa.'' Africa South, v.2, No.3, April-June
      1958: p.89-99.

459. ------,
      ''Islam and national movements in West Africa.''
      Journal of African History, v.3, 1962: p.323-327.
          Summary of a lecture given at the University
      of Boston which shows the influence of Islam on
      movements that seek to transform the colonial
      situation in Senegal and Chad.

460.   HODGKIN, Thomas
       ''Islam and national movements in West Africa.''
       In Africa from early times to 1800, edited by
       P.J.M. McEwan, New York, Oxford University Press,
       1968: p.361-367.

461.   ------,
       ''Islam and politics in West Africa.'' West
       Africa,   September 15-November 10, 1956.

462.   ------,
       ''Islam, history and politics.'' Journal of
       Modern African Studies, 1963: p.91-97.
           Review article on the History of Islam in
       West Africa, by J.S. Trimingham, London, 1962.

463.   ------,
       ''Islam in West Africa.'' Africa South, v.2,
       No.3, 1958: p.89-99.
           A historical account of the process of
       Islamization in West Africa (the Sudan) starting
       from the Almoravid invasion of the 11th century
       and gradual conversion of the negroes through
       peaceful means, proselytizing through the Sufi
       orders, and the events leading to the collapse
       of Sudanic empires by 1590.

464.   ------,
       The radical tradition in the literature of Muslim
       West Africa. London, (School of Oriental and
       African Studies, Seminar paper), 1968.

465. HUNWICK, J.O.
''The influence of Arabic in West Africa: a
preliminary survey.'' Transactions of the Historical Society of Ghana, v.7, 1964: p.24-41.
Islam brought to West Africa some knowledge
of the Arabic language and Muslim culture, which
introduced literacy and an improvement in communication through the use of a common language as
far back as the 11th century.

466. ------,
''Islam in West Africa, A.D. 1000-1800.'' In
Thousand years of West African History, edited
by J.F.A. Ajayi and I. Espie, Camden, N.J.,
Nelson, 1967: p.113-130.

467. ------,
''Some notes on the term 'zanj' and its derivatives
in a West African chronicle.'' Research Bulletin,
v.4, Nos. 1-2, December 1968: p.41-52.

468. JENKINS, R. G.
''The evolution of religious brotherhoods in
North and Northwest Africa, 1523-1900.'' In
John Ralph Willis, (ed). Studies in West African
Islamic history, vol.1, 1972.

469. KHAN, Sarwat
''Islam in West Africa.'' Islamic Review,
July 1952: p.12-19.

470. LAW, R.C.C.
''Contacts between the Mediterranean civilizations

470. LAW, R.C.C. (Contd.)
        and West Africa in pre-Islamic times.'' Lagos
        Notes and Records, v.1, No.1, June 1967: p.52-62.

471. LE CHATELIER, A.
        L'Islam dans l'Afrique occidentale, Paris, G.
        Steinheil, 1899. 422p.

472. LE GRIP, A.
        ''Aspects actuels de l'Islam en A.O.F.'' Afrique
        et Asie, v.24, 1953: p.6-20. v.25, 1954: p.43-61.

473. LEVTZION, Nehemia
        ''Patterns of Islamization in West Africa.'' In
        McCall, D.F. (and others) eds. Aspects of West
        African Islam. Boston, 1971: p.31-39.

474. LEWICKI, T.
        ''The food of the West African peoples in the
        middle ages according to Arabic sources.''
        Ethnografia Polska, v.7, 1963: p.31-191.

475. MAUNY, Raymond
        ''L'Afrique occidentale d'apres les auteurs
        arabes anciens, (666-977).'' Notes Africaines,
        v.40, 1948: p.6-7.

476. McCALL, Daniel F. and BENNETT, N.R.
        Aspects of West African Islam. Boston, African
        Studies Center, Boston University. 1971. xiv, 234p
        (Boston University Papers on Africa, no.5).
        Collection of papers dealing with aspects of
        the Islamic religion in West Africa especially

476.   McCALL, Daniel F. and BENNETT, N.R. (Contd.)

from the historical point of view. Mainly
concerned with Senegal, Nigeria and the Sudan.

477.   MOURADIAN, Jacques
''Note sur les alterations du nom de'Mohammad'
chez les Noirs islamisés de l'Afrique occidentale.''
Bulletin du Comité d'Etudes Historiques et
Scientifiques de l'A.O.F., v.21, No.3, 1938:
p.459-462.

478.   MOUSER, Bruce L.
Voyages and travels to the West Coast of Africa
before 1800; a checklist of materials available
in the English language in the Indiana University
libraries. Bloomington, Ind., Indiana University
Press, 1966.

479.   NIANE, D.T. and SURET-CAWALE, Jean
Histoire de l'Afrique occidentale. Conakry,
Edition du Ministère de l'education nationale de
la Republique de Guinée. 1960. 167p.

480.   al-NAGER, O.A.
''West Africa and the pilgrimage to the Holy
Places of Islam.'' Research Bulletin (Centre
of Arabic Documentation, Ibadan), v.2, No.1,
1966: p.37-38.

481.   O'BRIEN, Donal C.
''Towards an Islamic policy in French West Africa.''
Journal of African History, v.8, No.2, 1967:

481. O'BRIEN, Donal C. (Contd.)

p.303-316.

There was no single applicable French Islamic policy in West Africa. However, the French stimulated the spread of Islam not deliberately, but by such means as the use of arabic in relations with traditional rulers, using Muslims in negotiations, and the use of Muslim law.

482. OKAH, Jibril
''Islamic civilization in West Africa.'' Latitude v.1, July-September 1960: p.33-42. illus.

483. PAGEARD, Robert
''Contribution critique à la chronologie historique de l'ouest Africain.'' Journal de la Société des Africanistes, v.32, 1962: p.91-177.

484. PARRINDER, E.G.
''Islam in West Africa.'' In Religion in the Middle East, vol.2, edited by A.J. Arberry. New York, Cambridge University Press, 1969.

485. ------,
''Islam in West Africa.'' West African Review, v.31, No.397, December 1960: p.12-15.

486. ------,
''Islam and West African indigenous religions.'' Numen, v.6, No.2, 1959: p.130-141.

Discusses the relationship of Islam with West African traditional religions and their

486. PARRINDER, E. Geoffrey (Contd.)

cultural and social significance.

487. POULET, G.

Les Maures de l'Afrique occidentale francaise.
Paris, 1904.

488. PRICE, J.H.

''Islam in West Africa.'' Manchester Guardian,
v.4, No.6, July 1956.

489. PROST, André

''L'Islam en Afrique occidentale.'' Grands Lacs,
v.63, No.1, October 1947: p.11-19.

490. PRUSSIN, Labelle

''The architecture of Islam in West Africa.''
African Arts/Arts d'Afrique, v.1, No.2, (Winter
1968): p.32-35; p.70-74.

491. ------,

The impact of Islam on architecture in West Africa.
ASAP, 1967. 23p.

492. QUECHON, Martine

''Reflexions sur certain aspects du syncretisme
dans l'Islam ouest-africain.'' Cahiers d'Etudes
Africaines (Paris), v.11, No.42, February 1971:
p.206-230. Bibliog.

493. QUELLIEN, Alain

La politique musulmane dans l'Afrique occidentale

493. QUELLIEN, Alain (Contd.)

   francaise. Paris, Larose, 1910. viii, 278p.

494. REECK, Dorrell L.
   ''Islam in a West African chiefdom: an interpretation.'' Muslim World, v.62, No.3, 1972:
   p.183-194.

495. RODNEY, Walter
   A history of the Upper Guinea Coast, 1545-1800.
   Oxford, Clarendon Press, 1970. xiii, 283p.

496. SMITH, H.F.C.
   ''Islam in West Africa.'' Ibadan, v.15, March
   1963: p.31-33.

497. STEWART, Charles C.
   ''A new source on the book market in Morocco in
   1830 and Islamic scholarship in West Africa.''
   Hesperis-Tamuda (Rabat), v.11, 1970: p.209-246.
   illus.

498. TRIMINGHAM, John Spencer
   The Christian Church and Islam in West Africa.

   London, Student Christian Movement Press, 1955.
   55p. illus. (I.M.C. research pamphlets, no.3).

499. ------,
   The history of Islam in West Africa. New York,
   Oxford University Press, 1962.
      This book is not an attempt to write a history
   of West Africa, but to show the way in which Islam

499. TRIMINGHAM, John Spencer (Contd.)

spread and moulded the history of the Western
Sudan.

500. ------,

Islam in West Africa. Oxford, Clarendon Press,
1959. ix, 269p. map.

A study based on the religious life of West
African muslims, including the history of Islam
in the area and the interaction between the
Islamic religion and the African societies.

501. VAJDA, G.

''Contribution à la connaissance de la litterature arabe en Afrique occidentale.'' Journal de
la Société des Africanistes, v.20, No.2, 1950:
p.229-237.

502. WALKER, F.D.

''Islam and Christianity in West Africa.'' Moslem
World, April 1929: p.129-133.

503. WILLIS, John Ralph

''Jihad fi Sabil Allah: its doctrinal basis in
Islam and some aspects of its evolution in nine-
teenth-century West Africa.'' Journal of African
History, v.8, No.3, 1967: p.395-415.

Recurring Islamic revivalist movements are
partially explained by the inability of the Muslim
community in disarray to preserve Islam in ideal
form.

504. YOUNG, Herrick B.
     ''Islam in West Africa.'' <u>Moslem World</u>, v.36,
     No.3, July 1946: p.261-262.

DAHOMEY

505. MARTY, Paul
     <u>Etudes sur l'Islam au Dahomey</u>. Paris, Laroux,
     1926. 273p. illus (Revue du Monde Musulman).

506. MAUPOIL, Bernard
     ''Contribution a l'etude de l'origine musulmane
     de la geomancie dans le Bas-Dahomey.'' <u>Journal
     de la Société des Africanistes</u>, v.13, 1943:
     p.1-94.

507. ------,
     ''Contribution a l'etude de l'origine musulmane
     de la geomancie dans le Bas-Dahomey.'' Thèse
     complementaire, Doctorat d'Etat-Lettres. Universite
     de Paris, 1943.

508. TUBIANA, Marie-Jose
     ''Un document inedit sur les sultans du Wadday.''
     <u>Cahiers d'Etudes Africaines</u>, v.2, May 1960:
     p.49-112.

GAMBIA

509. FISHER, Humphrey
     ''Ahmadiyya in the Gambia, French territories and

509. FISHER, Humphrey (Contd.)

Liberia.'' West Africa, No.2320, January 1962:
p.93.

510. GIRARD, J.

''Note sur l'histoire traditionelle de la Haute
Casamance.'' Bulletin de l'Institut Fondamental
d'Afrique Noire, series B, v.28, 1966: p.540-554.

511. PRINS, P.

''L'Islam et les musulmans etrangers dans les
sultanats du Haut Oubangui.'' Renseignements
Coloniaux, 1907: p.136-142; p.162-173.

512. QUINN, Charlotte A.

''Niumi: a nineteenth century Mandingo Kingdom.''
Africa, v.38, 1968: p.443-455.

513. ------,

Mandingo Kingdoms of the Senegambia: traditiona-
lism, Islam and European expansion. London,
Longman, 1972. 211p. bibliog.

Three chapters in this book are devoted to
'The rise of Islam in the Gambia', Maba Diakhou
and the Muslim jihad and the 'secularization of
the jihad.'

514. ROCHE, Christian

''Un resistant oublié: Sunkaru Kamara Chef Malinke
de Casamance.'' Bulletin de l'Institut Fondamental
d'Afrique Noire, serie B, v.34, No.1, 1972: p.51-
66.

515. SANNEH, L.O.
      ''The Islamic education of an African child:
      stresses and tensions.'' In Geoffrey N. Brown
      and Mervyn Hiskett. Conflict and harmony in
      education in tropical Africa. London, Allen and
      Unwin, 1975: p.168-186.
           An account drawn from the author's experiences
      in the Gambia.

516. WASHINGTON, Captain
      ''Some account of Mohanmedu-Sisei; a Mandingo
      of Nyani-Maru on the Gambia.'' Journal of the
      Royal Geographical Society of London, v.8, 1838:
      p.448-454.

517. ZEMP, H.
      ''La legende des griots Malinkes.'' Cahiers d'
      Etudes Africaines, v.7, 1966: p.611-642.

GHANA

518. ANQUANDAH, James
      ''Influence of Islamic culture.'' Ghana Radio
      Review & T.V. Times, v.4, No.48, 24 January 1964.

519. BONNEL DE MEZIERES, M.
      ''Recherches de l'emplacement de Ghana (Fouilles
      à Koumbi et à Settah), et sur le site de Tekrour.'
      Memoire de l'Academie des Inscriptions et des
      Belles Lettres, v.13, 1920: p.128-131.

520. BRAIMAH, B.A.R.
''Islamic education in Ghana.'' Ghana Bulletin of Theology, v.4, No.5, December 1973: p.1-16.

521. BROWN, A. Addo-Aryee.
''Historical account of Mohammedanism in the Gold Coast.'' Gold Coast Review, v.3, No.2, 1927: p.195-197.
History of the origin and development of the Islamic religion in the Gold Coast.

522. DEBRUNNER, Hans W. and FISHER, H.
''Early Fanti Islam.'' Ghana Bulletin of Theology, v.1, No.7, December 1959: p.23-35: v.1, No.8, June 1960: p.13-

523. DESPLAGNES, L.
''Note sur l'emplacement des ruines de Ganna ou Gannata, ancienne capitale soudanaise anterieure à l'Islam.'' Bulletin de Sociologie et Geographie de l'Afrique Occidentale Francaise, v.1, 1907: p.298-301.

524. DRETKE, James P.
''The Islamic community in Accra (an historical survey).'' M.A. Thesis. Legon, University of Ghana. Institute of African Studies, 1965. 187p.
A thesis on the increasing growth of the muslim population of Accra as a result of the steady influx of immigrants into the city.

525. DRETKE, J.P.
''The muslim community in Accra: a historical survey.'' M.A. Thesis, University of Ghana, 1968. 187p.

526. FAGE, J.D.
''Ancient Ghana: a review of the evidence.'' Transactions of the Historical Society of Ghana, v.3, 1957: p.77-98.

527. FISHER, Humphrey J.
''Early Fante Islam.'' Ghana Bulletin of Theology, v.1, No.7, December 1959, v.1, No.8, June 1960.

528. ------,
''The planting of Ahmaddiyya in Ghana.'' West Africa, No.2226, 1960: p.121.
    A short account of the Ahmadiyya movement in Ghana.

529. GOODY, Jack
''A note on the penetration of Islam into the West of the Northern Territories of the Gold Coast. Transactions of the Gold Coast and Togoland Historical Society, v.1, 1953: p.45-46.

530. ------,
''Reform, renewal and resistance: a Mahdi in Northern Ghana.'' In African perspectives, edited by C. Allen and R.W. Johnson, New York, Cambridge University Press, 1970: p.143-156.

530. GOODY, Jack (Contd.)

   Examines the Mahdist movement of northern
   Ghana as an example of prophetic cult movements
   in West Africa signalling religious revival and
   reform.

531. GRINDALL, B.T.

   ''Islamic affiliations and urban adaptation: the
   Sisala migrant in Accra, Ghana.'' Africa, v.43,
   No.4, 1973: p.333-346. illus.,Bibliog.

532. HODGKIN, Thomas

   ''The Islamic literary tradition in Ghana.'' In
   Islam in tropical Africa: studies presented at
   and discussed at the 5th International African
   Seminar, Ahmadu Bello University, Zaria,
   January 1964. London, Oxford University Press,
   1966: p.442-460.

533. ''ISLAM in the Gold Coast.'' West Africa, Nos.18/25.
   December 1958: 240p.

534. KAMALI, S. A.

   ''Islamic views of other religious communities.''
   Ghana Bulletin of Theology, v.2, No.7, December
   1964: p.16-25; v.2, No.8, June 1965: p.17-27.

535. LEVTZION, Nehemia

   Ancient Ghana and Mali. London, Methuen, 1973.
   x, 283p. (Studies in African history, no.7).
   A full-length account of the ancient empires
   of Ghana and Mali based on the available evidence

535. LEVTZION, Nehemia (Contd.)

> from the chronides of black Muslim literati, existing oral traditions, and Arabic and Portuguese sources. It analyses the role of Islam in the royal courts, and in the commercial centers where scholarship sustained a more vigorous brand of Islam.

536. ------,

> ''Commerce et Islam chez les Dagomba du Nord-Ghana.'' Annales, Economies, Sociétés, Civilisations, July-August 1968: p.723-743.

537. ------,

> Muslims and chiefs in West Africa: a study of Islam in the Middle Volta Basin in the pre-colonial period. Oxford, Clarendon Press, 1968. 228p.

538. ------,

> The spread and the development of Islam in the middle Volta Basin in the pre-colonial period. London, University Press, 1965.

539. ------,

> ''The spread and development of Islam in the Middle Volta Basin in the pre-colonial period.'' Ph.D. Thesis. University of London, 1965.

540. LOCHMAN, A.J.

> ''Early Fante Islam.'' Ghana Bulletin of Theology v.1, No.7, December 1959: p.23-35; v.1, No.8, 1960: p.13-29.

541. MORO, A.B.I.
The impact of the Haj in Yendi.2. Islamic
scholarship in Yendi. Inter-disciplinary seminar
in field methods, summer 1968. Legon, Institute
of African studies, and Northwestern University
Program of African Studies, 1968. (Yendi project,
No.7).

542. ODOOM, K.O.
''A document on pioneers of the Muslim community
in Accra.'' Research Review, (Institute of
African Studies, Legon), v.7, No.3, 1971: p.1-31.

543. ------,
Muslim marriage among the Dagombas. Legon, Accra,
University of Ghana, Institute of African Studies,
1972.

544. ------,
Islamic education in Yendi. Interdisciplinary
seminar in field methods, summer 1968, Legon,
Institute of African Studies, and Northwestern
University Program of African Studies, 1968.
(Yendi Project No.8).

545. OPPONG, Christine
Growing up in Dagbon. Accra-Tema, Ghana Publi-
shing Corporation, 1973. 79p. bibliog. illus.
An account of the context and content of
education of children in the Northern Ghana
kingdom of Dagbon based on material collected
for M.A. thesis. Parts of the work deal with
the nature of muslim education in Northern Ghana -
how to become a Mallam or a Diviner.

546. PRICE, J.H.

''The role of Islam in Gold Coast politics.''
West African Institute of Social and Economic
Research. Annual Conference. March 1954. p.104-111

547. SIDIKI, Abdulai

''The role of traders in the spread of Islam in
Wa, Salaga and Kumasi.'' Unpublished B.A. Honours
Dissertation, Department of History, University
of Ghana, 1972. 20p.

548. SOLKEN, Heinz

''Zur biographie des Imam Umaru von Kete-Kratyi.''
Africana Marburgensia, vol.3, No.2, 1970: p.24-29.

549. STEVENS, Phyllis

The organisation of Islam in Yendi. Interdisciplinary seminar in field methods, summer 1968.
Institute of African Studies, Ghana and Programme
of African Studies, Northwestern University, U.S.A
1968. (unpaged) (Yendi Project No.10).

550. STEWART, C.C.

''The Tijaniya in Ghana; a historical study.''
M.A. Thesis. Legon, University of Ghana, Institute of African Studies, v.1, 85p.

551. THOMASSEY, P. and MAUNY, R.

Campagne de fouilles de 1950 à Koumbi Saleh
(Ghana?). Bulletin de l'Institut Fondamental d'
Afrique Noire, series B, v.28, 1956: p.117-140.

552. VIDAL, J.

''La mystere de Ghana.'' Bulletin du Comité d'
Etudes Historiques et Scientifiques de l'Afrique
Occidentale Francaise, vo.6, 1923: p.512-524.

553. WILKS, I.

''The growth of Islamic learning in Ghana.''
Journal of the Historical Society of Nigeria, v.2,
No.4, December 1963: p.409-417.

By the mid-18th century, Islamic learning was
firmly established with a tradition of local
authorship in the field of historiography and a
learned centre at Bouna on the western frontier
of Gonja.

554. ------,

''Islam in Ghana history: an outline.'' Ghana
Bulletin of Theology, v.2, 1962: p.20-28.

A note on the spread of Islam into modern
Ghana from the 14th century to the 19th century.

555. ------,

Muslim office in Dagomba. Inter-disciplinary
seminar in field methods. Summer, 1968. Institute
of African Studies, Ghana and Programme of African
Studies, North-western University, U.S.A. 1968.
(unpaged) (Yendi Project No.11).

556. ------,

''A note on the early spread of Islam in Dagomba.''
Transactions of the Historical Society of Ghana,
v.8, 1965: p.87-98.

557. WILKS, Ivor
''The position of Muslims in Metropolitan Ashanti
in the early nineteenth century.'' Journal of the
Historical Society of Nigeria, v.2, No.4, December
1963: p.318-339. Also in Islam in Tropical Africa,
edited by I.M. Lewis. London, Oxford University
Press, 1966: p.318-341.

558. ------,
The position of Muslims in metropolitan Ashanti
in the early nineteenth century. Legon, Institute
of African Studies, University of Ghana, 1963.
28p. illus.

559. ------,
''The Saghanughu and the spread of Maliki law:
a provisional note.'' Research Bulletin (Legon),
v.2, No.2, July 1966: p.11-19.

560. ------,
The tradition of Islamic learning in Ghana. Accra
University of Ghana, 1962. 5p.

GUINEA

561. BEYRIES, J.
''L'Islam en Guinee francaise.'' Memoires. Centre
des Hautes Etudes d'Administration Musulmane,
No.2538, 1958.

562. CARREIRA, Antonio
Aspectos historicos de evolucado do Islamismo na
Guiné Portuguesa (Achegas para o seu estudo)

562. CARREIRA, Antonio (Contd.)

Boletim cultural da de Guine Portuguesa (Bissau),
v.21, No.84, October 1966: p.405-455.

563. GONCALVES, Jose Julio
O. Islamismo na Guine portuguesa. Lisboa,
Agencia Geral do Ultramar, 1961. 222p.

564. HARRIS, Joseph
''The Foula of Fouta Diallon: their origin,
migration, and religion;'' paper read at the
Second International Conference of Africanists,
Dakar, December 1967.

565. HOLDEN, Jeff
''The Samorian impact on Buna: an essay in metho-
dology.'' In Allen, Christopher and Johnson,
R.W. (eds). African perspectives: papers in the
history, politics and economics of Africa presented
to Thomas Hodgkin. Cambridge, University Press,
1970: p.83-108.

566. HOPEWELL, James Franklin
Muslim penetration into French Guinea, Sierra
Leone, and Liberia before 1850. Ann Arbor, Mich.
University Microfilms, 1958.

567. KOUROUBARI, A.
''Histoire de l'Imam Samori.'' Bulletin de l'
Institut Fondamental d'Afrique Noire, series B.
V.21, 1959: p.544-571.

568. LEVTZION, Nehemia

Mahmud Ka'ti fut-il l'auteur de Tarikh al-Fattash?
Bulletin de l'Institut Fondamental d'Afrique Noire
v.33, Serie B, No.4, 1971: p.666-674.

569. ------,

"Notes sur l'origine de l'Islam militant au
Fouta-Djalon." Notes Africains de l'I.F.A.N.,
v.132, October 1971: p.94-96.

570. MARTY, Paul

"L'Islam en Guinée: Fouta-Diallon." Revue du
Monde musulman, v.36, 1918-19: p.160-227.

571. MARTY, Paul and SAYERS, Eldred F.

"Islam in French Guinea." Sierra Leone Studies,
No.19, December 1933: p.47-129. No.20 December
1936: p.5-66; No.21, January 1939: p.119-205.

572. NIANE, Djibril Tamsir

"Mythes, legendes et sources orales dans l'oeuvre
de Mahmoud Kati." Recherches Africaines (Conakry)
1964: p.1-4, 1966: p.36-42.

573. PERSON, Y.

"Les ancestres de Samori." Cahiers d'Etudes
Africaines, v.4, 1963: p.125-156.

574. RICHARD-MOLLARD, J.

"Islam ou colonisation au Fouta-Diallon? Propos
d'un geographe l'apel du monde paien." Missions
Evangeliques, October 1943: p.17-24.

575. RIVIERE, Claude
    ''Bilan de l'islamisation en Guinée.'' Afrique
    Documents (Dakar) Nos. 105/106. 1969: p.319-359.

576. ROBINSON, David
    ''Abdul Bokar Kan and the history of the Futa
    Toro, 1854-1891.'' Ph.D. Thesis, Columbia
    University, New York, 1970.

577. ------,
    ''Abdul Qadir and Shaykh Umar: a continuing
    tradition of Islamic leadership in Futa Toro.''
    International Journal of African Historical
    Studies, v.6, No.2, 1973: p.286-304.

578. SAINT-PERE
    ''Creation du royaume du Fouta Djalon.'' Bulletin
    du Comité d'Etudes Historiques et Scientifique de
    l'Afrique Occidentale Francaise, v.12, 1929:
    p.484-555.

579. SOW, Alfa Ibrahim
    Chroniques et recits du Fouta Djalon. Paris,
    1968.

580. SURET-CANALE, Jean
    ''Touba in Guinea - Holy place of Islam.'' In
    Allen, Christopher and Johnson, R.W. (eds).
    African perspectives: papers in the history,
    politics and economics of Africa presented to
    Thomas Hodgkin. Cambridge, University Press,
    1970: p.53-81.

581. WANE, Yaya

''De Halwaar à Degembere ou l'itineraire Islamique de Shaykh Umar Taal.'' Bulletin IFAN (Dakar), v.31, (B) No.2, April 1969: p.445-451.

IVORY COAST

582. BENQUEY,

''Considerations sur l'Islam Africain (Haute Côte d'Ivoire).'' Bulletin du Comité d'Etudes Historiques et Scientifique de l'Afrique Occidentale Francaise. 1921: p.678-688.

583. COUTY, Philippe et al.

Entretiens avec des marabouts et des paysans du Baol. Dakar-Hann, Centre ORSTOM, 1968. 79p.

584. FADIKA, Mamadou

''Les droits, les sorciers, magiciens, guerisseurs feticheurs et Marabouts.'' Revue Ivoirienne de Droit. Nos. 1/2, 1972/73: p.45-50.

585. HOLAS, B.

''La Goumbe: une association de jeunne musulmane en base Cote d'Ivoire.'' Kongo-Overzee, v.19, No.2/3, 1953: p.116-131.

586. MARTY, Paul

Etudes sur l'Islam en Côte d'Ivoire. Paris, Leroux, 1922. 496p. illus.

587. TRIAUD, Jean-Louis
      ''Un cas de passage collectif à l'Islam en Basse
      Côte d'Ivoire: le village d'Ahua ou debut du
      siècle.'' Cahiers d'Etudes Africaines, v.14,
      No.2, 1974: p.317-337.
          Ahua is a Baule village on the Bandama river,
      Ivory Coast. This is an account of the massive
      conversion of the inhabitants of this village
      into the Islamic faith.

588. ------,
      ''La penetration de l'Islam en Cote d'Ivoire:
      notes et documents pour servir à l'histoire des
      Musulmans de Côte meridionale (1900-1935).''
      These, 3e cycle. Université de Paris. 1971.
      674p. typescript.

LIBERIA

589. EARTHY, E. Dora
      ''The impact of Mohammedanism on paganism in the
      Liberian hinterland.'' Numen, v.2, No.3,
      September 1955: p.206-216.

MALI

590. BARTH, Heinrich
      ''Al-Hajj Bashir, Kukawa, and Timbuktu.'' In
      Robert O. Collins, (ed). African history: text
      and readings. New York, Random House, 1971:
      p.84-90.

591. BECKINGHAM, C.F.
      ''The pilgrimage and the death of Sakura, king
      of Mali.'' Bulletin of the School of Oriental
      and African Studies, v.15, 1953: p.391-392.

592. BELL, N.
      ''The age of Mansa Musa of Mali: problems in
      succession and chronology.'' Conference on
      Manding Studies, School of Oriental and African
      Studies. London, 1972. unpublished.

593. BROWN, W.A.
      ''The Bakka'iyya books of Timbuktu (Kunta).''
      Research Bulletin (Centre of Arabic Documentation,
      Ibadan), v.3, No.1, January 1967: p.40-44.

594. CEPOLLARO, Armando.
      ''La figura de Sundiata Keita nella tradizione
      orale e nei documenti scritti.'' Africa (Rome)
      June 1967: p.171-197.

595. CHAILEY, M.
      ''Aspects de l'Islam au Mali.'' In Notes et
      études sur l'Islam en Afrique noire. Paris,
      1962: p.9-52.

596. CISSOKO, S.M.
      ''L'intelligentsia de Timbouctou aux XVe et XVIe
      siècles.'' Présence Africaine, No.72, 1969:
      p.48-72. Also in Bulletin de l'Institut Fondamen-
      tal d'Afrique Noire, serie B, No.4, 1969: p.927-
      952.

597. CISSOKO, Sekene Mody
      ''Le siècle de Kankou Moussa: le XIVe siècle.''
      Présence Africaine, No.52, 1964: p.94-103.

598. DESIRE-VUILLEMIN, Genevieve M.
      Kango Moussa, empereur du Mali. Realisé par le
      S.E.R.P.E.D. avec la collaboration de Genevieve
      Desire-Vuillemin. Paris, Institut Pedagogique
      national, 1963. (Documentation pedagogique
      africaine, no.2).

599. DUBOIS, Felix
      Tombouctou la mysterieuse. Paris, Flammarion,
      1896. 380p.

600. GAILLARD, M.
      ''Niani, ancienne capitale de l'empire Mandingue.''
      Bulletin d'Etudes Historiques et Scientifiques de
      l'Afrique Occidentale Francaise, v.6, 1923:
      p.620-636.

601. HAMPATE BA, Amadou
      ''Des Foulbe du Mali et de leur culture.''
      Abbia (Yaounde), v.14/15, July-December, 1966:
      p.23-54.

602. HAMPATE BA, Amadou and DAGET, J.
      L'empire peul du Macina. Bamako, Institut
      Francais d'Afrique Noire, Centre du Soudan, 1955.
      (Etudes Soudanaises, no.3).

603. HAMPATE BA, Ahmadu
''Sheik Ahmadu and Masina.'' In Robert O. Collins (ed). African history: text and readings. New York, Random House, 1971: p.90-98.

604. HERVE, H.
''Niani, ex-capitale de l'empire mandingue.'' Notes Africaines, No.82, 1959: p.51-55.

605. HUMBLOT, P.
''Episodes de la legende de Soundjata.'' Notes Africaines, No.52, 1951: p.111-113.

606. HUNWICK, J.O.
''Ahmad Baba and the Moroccan invasion of the Sudan - 1591.'' Journal of the Historical Society of Nigeria, v.2, No.3, 1962: p.311-328.

607. ------,
''An Andalusian in Mali: a contribution to the biography of Abu Ishaq al-Sahili, c.1290-1346.'' Conference on Manding Studies, School of Oriental and African Studies, London, 1972. (unpublished)

608. ------,
''Further light on Ahmad Baba al-Timbukti.'' Research Bulletin (Centre of Arabic Documentation Ibadan), v.2, No.2, 1966: p.19-31.

609. ------,
''The mid-fourteenth century capital of Mali.'' Conference on Manding Studies, School of Oriental and African Studies, London, 1972. (unpublished)

610. HUNWICK, J.O.

''A new source of the biography of Ahmad Baba
al-Tinbukti (1556-1627).'' Bulletin of the
School of Oriental and African Studies, v.27,
No.3, 1964: p.568-593.

611. JACKSON, J.G.

An account of Timbuctoo and Housa by el Hage Abd
Salam Shabeeny. London, Printed for Longman,
Hurst, Rees, Orme and Brown. 1820.

612. JACOBS, J.

''Les epopées de Soundjata et de Chaka; une étude
comparée.'' Aequatoria, v.25, No.4, 1962: p.121-
124.

613. LEVTZION, N.

''The thirteenth - and fourteenth century kings
of Mali.'' Journal of African History, v.4, 1963:
p.341-353.

614. MARO-SCHRADER, L.

''Tombouctou et le trafic saharien.'' Revue de
Paris, 15 March 1962: p.307-310.

615. MEILLASSOUX, C.

''Beexamen de l'itineraire d'Ibn Battuta entre
Walata et Malli.'' Conference on Manding Studies,
School of Oriental and African Studies, London,
1972. (unpublished)

616. MEILLASSOUX, C.
   ''Le commerce pre-colonial et le developpement
   de l'esclavage à Gumbu du Sahel (Mali).''
   L'Homme et la Société, 1970: p.147-157.

617. MONTEIL, Charles
   L'oeuvre des etrangers dans l'empire soudanais
   du Mali.'' Revue des Etudes Islamiques, v.3,
   1929: p.227-235.

618. MONTRAT, M.
   ''Notice sur l'emplacement de l'ancienne capitale
   du Mali.'' Notes Africaines, No.79, 1958: p.90-93

619. NIANE, Djibril Tamsir
   ''Niani, capitale de l'empire du Mali.'' Paper
   read at the Second International Congress of
   Africanists. Dakar, 1967.

620. ------,
   ''Le probleme des Soundjata.'' Notes Africaines,
   v.88, 1960: p.123-126.

621. ------,

   Recherches sur l'empire du Mali au Moyen-Age.
   Diplome d'etudes superieures soutenu a la Faculté
   des Lettres de Bordeaux. Conakry: Republique de
   Guinée, Ministere de l'Information et du Tourisme,
   1962.

622. ------,

   Sundiata: an epic of old Mali. Translated by D.G.
   Pickett. London, Longmans, 1965. x, 96p.

623. NIANE, D.T.

Soundjata_ou_l'epopee_Mandigue. 2nd ed., Paris, Présence Africaine, 1960. 154p. illus.

624. NORRIS, H.T.

''Sanhajah scholars of Timbuctoo.'' Bulletin_of the_School_of_Oreintal_and_African_Studies, v.30, No.3, 1967: p.634-640.

625. PAGEARD, Robert

''La marche orientale du Mali (Segou-Djenne) en 1644, d'apres le Tarikh Es-Soudan.'' Journal_de la_Société_des_Africanistes, v.31, 1961: p.73-90.

626. ------,

''Soundiata Keita et la tradition orale.'' Présence_Africaine, No.36, 1961: p.51-70.

627. PERSON, Y.

''Nyani Mansa Mamudu et la fin de l'empire du Mali.'' Conference on Manding Studies, School of Oriental and African Studies. London, 1972. (unpublished)

628. POL-PAGES

''Le Mahometisme dans le 'Hombori' en 1922. (Region de Tombouctou-Soudan Francais).'' Bulletin_du_Comité_d'Etudes_Historiques_et Scientifiques_de_l'A.O.F., v.16, No.3, July-September 1933: p.360-410.

629. SHELTON, A.S.

''The problem of griot interpretation and the actual causes of war in Sundjata.'' Présence Africaine, No.66, 1968: p.145-152.

630. SIDIBE, M.

''Soundiata Keita, heros historique et legendaire, empereur du Manding.'' Notes Africaines, No.82, 1959: p.41-51.

631. TRIAUD, Jean-Louis

''La lutte entre la Tidjaniya et la Qadriya dans le Macina au 19e siecle.'' Annales de l'Université d'Abidjan, Series F.1, No.1, 1969: p.149-171. Bibliog.

632. ------,

''Quelques remarques sur l'islamisation du Mali, des origines à 1300.'' Bulletin de l'Institut Fondamental d'Afrique Noire, v.30, series B, 1968: p.1329-1352.

633. ------,

''Quelques remarques sur l'islamisation du Mali au dix-neuvième siècle.'' Annales de l'Université d'Abidjan, Serie F.1, Fasc.1, 1969: p.149-171.

634. VIDAL, J.

''La legende officielle de Soundjata.'' Bulletin du Comité d'Etudes Historiques et Scientifique de l'Afrique Occidentale Francaise, v.7, 1924: p.317-328.

MALI

635. VIDAL, J.

''Au sujet de l'emplacement du Mali.'' Bulletin
du Comité d'Etudes Historiques et Scientifiques
de l'Afrique Occidentale Francaise, v.6, 1923:
p.251-268.

MAURITANIA

636. BENACHENON, A.

''Sidi 'Abd Allah Moul l'-Gara ou Abdallah Ibn
Yasin.'' Hesperis, v.33, 1946: p.406-413.

637. CURTIN, Philip D.

''Jihad in West Africa: early phases and their
relations in Mauritania and Senegal.'' Journal
of African History, v.12, No.1, 1971: p.11-24.

638. DESIRE-VUILLEMIN, Genevieve M.

Contribution à l'histoire de la Mauritanie de
1900 à 1934. Dakar, Editions Clairafrique, 1962.
412p.

639. DESIRE-VUILLEMIN, G.M., and others.

Histoire de la Mauritanie des origines au milieu
du XVIIIe siècle, par G.M. Desire-Vuillemin, avec
la participation de Mohammed el Chennafi, Mokhtar
Ould Hamidoun et Elimane Kane. Nouackenolt,
Ministere de l'Education et de la jeuneusse,
Republique Islamique de Mauritanie, 1964. illus.

115

640. DESIRE-VUILLEMIN, Genevieve M.
Les rapports de la Mauritanie et du Maroc. Edité
par le Service des archives nationales de Mauritanie à l'occasion de la Proclamation de l'indepen-
dance de la Republique Islamique de 28 Novembre
1960. Saint-Louis, 1960. 38p.

641. HAMET, Ismael
Chroniques de la Mauritanie senegalaise. Paris,
1911.

642. LAFORGUE, Pierre
''Une secte heresiarque en Mautanie: Les 'Ghoudf.'
Bulletin du Comité d'Etudes Historiques et Scien-
tifiques de l'AOF., v.11, No.4, 1928: p.654-665.

643. LEMOYNE, Robert
''Enquete sur le droit penal local de la Mauritani
Archives, Institut Fondamental d'Afrique Noire,
v.13, No.6, 1938.

644. LERICHE, A.
''Notes sur les classes sociale et sur quelques
tribus de Mauritanie.'' Bulletin de l'Institut
Fondamental d'Afrique Noire, v.17, serie B, Nos.
1/2, 1955: p.173-203.

645. MARTY, Paul
''Les Ida ou Ali, Chorfa de Mauritanie.'' Revue
du Monde Musulmane, v.31, 1915-16: p.221-274.

646. MARTY, Paul

L'islam en Mauritanie et en Senegal. Paris,
Leroux, 1915-16. 848p. (Collection Revue du Monde
musulman.)

647. MEUNIE, D. Jacques

''Cité caravanieres de Mauritanie: Tichite et
Oualata.'' Journal de la Societe des Africanistes,
v.27, 1957: p.19-35.

648. MISKE, Ahmad-Baba

Al-Wasit (1911), tableau de la Mauritanie à la
fin du XIXe siècle. Bulletin, I.F.A.N., v.30, serie
B, No.1, 1968: p.117-164.

649. NORRIS, H.T.

''Znaga Islam during the seventeenth and eighteenth
centuries.'' Bulletin of the School of Oriental
and African Studies, v.32, No.3, 1969: p.496-526.

650. al-SHINQITI, Ahmad Ibn al-Amin

El Wasit; litterature, histoire, geographie,
moeurs et coutumes des habitants de la Mauritanie.
Extraits traduits de l'arabe par Mourad Teffahi.
Saint Louis, Senegal, Centre IFAN - Mauritanie,
1953.

651. STEWART, C.C.

''A new document concerning the origins of the
Awalad Ibiri and the N'tishait.'' Bulletin de
l'Institut Fondamental d'Afrique Noire, v.31,
No.1, 1969: p.309-319.

652.   STEWART, C.C.
       ''Political authority and social stratification
       in Mauritania.'' In Arab-Berber relations: a
       survey of ethnic group relations in North Africa,
       edited by C. Micaud & E. Gellner. London, 1973.

653.   ------,
       ''The role of Shaikh Sidiyya and the Qadiriyya in
       Southern Mauritania: an historical interpretation
       D. Phil. Thesis, Oxford University, 1970.

654.   STEWART, C.C. and STEWART, E.K.
       Islam and social order in Mauretania: a case
       study from the nineteenth century. Oxford,
       Clarendon Press, 1973. 204p.
           This book seeks to explain the contribution
       of Shaikh Sidiyya al–Kabir (1775-1868) to the
       theory and application of Islamic law and the
       influence of his juridical studies on the 'scienc
       of mysticism among the nomadic societies of
       Mauritania.

655.   TOUPET, C.
       ''Les grands traits de la republique islamique
       de Mauritanie.'' L'information geographique,
       1962: p.47-56.

656. ABDUL MALIKI, H.E. Alhaji
       ''Islam in Nigeria.'' Islamic Quarterly, v.9,
       1965: p.30-36.

657. ABDUL, M.O.A.
       ''Syncretism in Islam among the Yoruba.'' West
       African Religion, v.15, March 1974: p.44-56.

658. ------,
       ''Yoruba divination and Islam.'' Orita, v.4,
       No.1, June 1970: p.17-25.

659. ADEBAYO, D.
       ''Daura: the cradle of the Hausa race.''
       Nigerian Citizen, February 1962.

660. ADELEYE, R.A.
       ''The dilemma of the Wazir: the place of the
       'Risalat al-Wazir ila ahl al-ilm wa l-taddabur'
       in the history of the Sokoto caliphate.''
       Journal of the Historical Society of Nigeria,
       v.4, No.2, 1968.
            Text in Arabic and English.

661. ------
       Power and diplomacy in Northern Nigeria 1804-1906:
       the Sokoto Caliphate and its enemies. London,
       Longman, 1971. xvi, 387p. illus., bibliog.
            The first chapter covers the jihad of Uthman
       Dan Fodio and the growth of Islam.

662. ADELEYE, R.A. et al
     ''Sifofin Shehu: an autobiography and character
     study of 'Uthman b. Fudi in verse.'' Bulletin,
     Centre of Arabic Documentation, (Ibadan), v.2,
     No.1, 1966.

663. AL-HAJJ, Muhammad A.
     "The Fulani concept of Jihad; Shehu Uthman dan
     Fodio." Odu, v.1, No.1. July 1964: p.45-58.
         A study which demonstrates that the Fulani
     jihad was essentially a religious upheaval
     provoked by the Islamic Fulanis against the
     pagan Hausa rulers.

664. ------,
     ''The thirteenth century in Muslim eschatology:
     Mahdist expectations in the Sokoto caliphate.''
     Research Bulletin. (Centre for Arabic Documenta-
     tion, Ibadan), v.3, No.2, July 1967: p.100-115.

665. AL-HAJJ, M.A. and LAST, D.M.
     ''Attempts at defining a Muslim in 19th century
     Hausaland and Bornu.'' Journal of the Historical
     Society of Nigeria, v.3, No.2, 1965: p.231-240.

666. AL-KANAMI, Muhammad
     ''The case against the jihad.'' In Thomas
     Hodgkin, Nigerian perspectives, an historical
     anthology. London, Oxford University Press, 1960:
     p.198-201. Also in Robert O. Collins (ed.)
     African history: text and readings, New York,
     Random House, 1971: p.67-69.

667.   ALLEN, Edmund Woods
       The travels of Abdul Karim in Hausaland and Bornu.
       Zaria, (Nigeria). N.R.L.A. 1958.

668.   ANJORIN, A.O.
       ''British occupation and development of Northern
       Nigeria: 1897-1914.'' Ph.D. Thesis, London
       University, 1965.

669.   BACKWELL, H.F. ed.
       The occupation of Hausaland 1900-1904, being a
       translation of Arabic letters found in the house
       of Wazir of Sokoto, Bohari in 1903. A new edition
       with an introductory note by M. Hiskett. London,
       Frank Cass, 1969. 80p. (Cass library of African
       Studies, General Studies, No.79).

670.   BALA ABUJA, J.
       ''Koranic and Moslem law teaching in Hausaland.''
       Nigeria, v.37, 1951: p.25-28.

671.   BALOGUN, I.A.B.
       ''The introduction of Islam into the Etsako
       Division of the Mid-Western state of Nigeria.''
       Orita, v.6, No.1, June 1972: p.26-38.

672.   --------,
       The penetration of Islam into Nigeria. Khartoum,
       University of Khartoum. Sudan Research Unit, 1969.
       (African Studies Seminar paper no.7).

673.   BARKOW, J.H.
       ''Hausa women and Islam.'' Canadian Journal of

673. BARKOW, J.H. (Contd.)

African Studies, v.6, No.2, 1972: p.317-328.

674. ------,

''Muslims and Maguzawa in North Central State,
Nigeria: an ethnographic comparison.'' Canadian
Journal of African Studies, v.7, No.1, 1973:
p.59-76.

675. BEIER, Ulli

''Sacred Yoruba architecture. I. Modern Islamic
architecture.'' Nigeria Magazine, No.64, March
1960: p.93-104. illus.

676. BELO, Muhammad

''The character of Shehu.'' In Thomas Hodgkin,
Nigerian perspectives, an historical anthology.
London, Oxford University Press, 1960: p.196-198.

677. BENTON, P.A.

The sultanate of Bornu. Translated from the
German of Dr. A. Schultze with additions and
appendices by P.A. Benton. London, Frank Cass,
1968. (Cass library of African Studies. General
Studies, No.50).

678. BIVAR, A.D.H.

''The Wathiqat ahl al-Sudan: a manifesto of the
Fulani jihad.'' Journal of African History, v.2,
No.2, 1961: p.235-243.

NIGERIA

679. BOVILL, E.W.
''The Niger and the Songhai empire.'' Journal
of the African Society, v.25, 1925-1926: p.138-148.

680. BRAUKAMPER, Ulrich
Der einfluss des Islam auf die Geschichte und
kulturentwicklung Adamauas. Abriss eines Afrikani-
schen kulturwandels. Wiesbaden, Franz Steiner,
1970. 223p. (Studien zur kulturkunde, 26).
A historical study which attempts to present
and assess the process of Islamization and the
Islamic influence on the development of Adamawa
culture.

681. BRENNER, Louis
The Shehus of Kukawa: a history of the Al-Kanemi
dynasty of Bornu. Oxford, Clarendon Press, 1973.
A general political history of nineteenth-
century Bornu with emphasis upon the description
and analysis of internal dynamics within the
ruling classes of Bornu.

682. ''BRITISH policy and Islam in Southern Nigeria.''
Moslem World, v.1, 1911: p.296-300.

683. COHEN, Ronald
''The Bornu king lists.'' Boston University
Papers on Africa, v.2, African history, edited
by Jeffrey Butler. Boston, Boston University
Press, 1966: p.41-83.

123

NIGERIA

684. COHEN, Ronald
Dominance and defiance: a study of marital insta-
bility in an Islamic African society (Kanuri).
Washington, American Anthropological Association,
1971, xix, 213p. bibliog. illus.

685. ------,
''The dynamics of feudalism in Bornu.'' In
Boston University Papers on Africa. Vol.II of
African history. Edited by Jeffrey Butler. Boston,
Boston University Press, 1966: p.87-105.

686. ------,
''From empire to colony: Bornu in the nineteenth
and twentieth centuries.'' In V. Turner, (ed).
Colonialism in Africa, 1870-1970. v.3, Profiles
of change: African Society and Colonial rule.
Cambridge, Cambridge University Press, 1971.

687. ------,
The Kanuri of Bornu. New York, Holt, Rinehart
and Winston, 1967.

688. ------,
''Power, authority, and personal success in Islam
and Bornu.'' In M. Swartz (and others) (eds).
Political anthropology. Chicago, Aldine, 1966.

689. ------,
''The structure of Kanuri society.'' Ph.D.
Thesis, University of Wisconsin, 1960.

124

690. CROWDER, M.

''Islam in Northern Nigeria.'' <u>Geographical</u>
<u>Magazine</u>, October 1958: p.304-316.

691. DAMANN, Ernst

''Muhammed bin Abubekr bin Omar Kidjumwa Masihii.''
<u>Afrika und U bersee</u>, v.52, Nos. 3/4, June 1969:
p.314-321.

692. DAN FODIO, Abdullah

''The intellectual background to the Fulani jihad.''
<u>In</u> Thomas Hodgkin, <u>Nigerian perspectives: an</u>
<u>historical anthology</u>. London, Oxford University
Press, 1960: p.188-190.

693. DAN FODIO, Uthman

''The origins of the Fulani jihad.'' <u>In</u> Thomas
Hodgkin, <u>Nigerian perspectives: an historical</u>
<u>anthology</u>. London, Oxford University Press,
1960: p.191-194.

694. DANIEL, F.

''Shehu Dan Fodio.'' <u>Journal of the African</u>
<u>Society</u>, v.25, No.99, April 1926: p.278-283.

695. DENHAM, Dixon

''Bornu and Sheik al-Kanami.'' <u>In</u> Robert O.
Collins (ed). <u>African history: text and readings.</u>
New York, Random House, 1971: p.72-78.

696. DENHAM, Dixon <u>and</u> CLAPPERTON, Hugh

''Muhammad al-Kanami: the ruler, the poet, the
diplomat.'' <u>In</u> Thomas Hodgkin, <u>Nigerian perspec-</u>

696. DENHAM, Dixon and CLAPPERTON, Hugh (Contd.)

tives, an historical anthropology. London,
Oxford University Press, 1960: p.205-209.

697. DE SEETZEN, M.
''Nouveaux renseignements sur les Royaume ou
Empire de Bornou, recueillis au Caire.'' Annales
des voyages, v.19, 1812: p.164-184.

698. DIANOUX, H.J. de.
''Les mots d'emprunts d'origine arabe dans la
langue Songhay.'' Bulletin de l'Institut Fondamental de l'Afrique Noire, v.23, Nos. 3/4, 1961:
p.596-606.

699. DOI, A.R.I.
''An aspect of Islamic syncretism in Yorubaland.''
Orita, v.5, No.1, June 1971: p.36-45.

700. ------,
''The Bamidele movement in Yorubaland.'' Orita,
v.3, No.2, December 1969: p.101-118.

701. ------,
''A Muslim-Christian-traditional saint in Yorubaland.'' (Bilikisu Sungbo) Practical Anthropology, v.17, No.6, November-December, 1970:

p.261-268.

702. ------,
''The Yoruba Mahdi.'' Journal of Religions in
Africa (Leiden), v.4, No.2, p.119-138.

NIGERIA

703. DRY, D.P.L.
      ''The place of Islam in Hausa society.''
      D.Phil. Thesis, Oxford University, 1952-53.

704. FARRANT, H.G.
      ''Northern Nigerian opportunity.'' Moslem World,
      October 1937: p.337-347.

705. FISHER, Humphrey J.
      ''The Ahmadiyya movement in Nigeria.'' African
      Affairs, v.1, 1961: p.60-88.

706. ------,
      ''Independency and Islam: the Nigerian Aladuras
      and some Muslim comparisons: review article.''
      (books by J.D.Y. Peel and H.W. Turner) Journal
      of African History (London), v.11, No.2, 1970:
      p.269-277.

707. FREMANTLE, J.M.
      ''History of the region comprising the Katagum
      division of Kano province.'' Journal of the
      African Society, v.10, Nos. 29 & 40, 1910-11.

708. GBADOMASI, G.O.
      ''The establishment of Western education among
      muslims in Nigeria, 1896-1926.'' Journal of the
      Historical Society of Nigeria, v.4, No.1, December
      1967.

709. ------,
      ''The growth of Islam among the Yoruba, 1841-1908.'
      Ph.D. thesis, University of Ibadan, 1968: p.252.

710.   GERVIS, Pearce

Of emirs and pagans: a view of Northern Nigeria.
London, Cassell, 1963. xvi, 210p. illus.

711.   GOERNER, Margaret (and others)

''Two essays on Arabic loan words in Hausa.''
Zaria, (Northern Nigeria) Dept. of Languages,
Ahmadu Bello University, 1966. (Occasional paper
No.7).

712.   GREENBERG, J.H.

''Arabic loan words in Hausa.'' Word, v.3, 1947:
p.85-97.

713.   ------,

The influence of Islam on a Sudanese religion.
New York, Augustin, 1946. ix, 73p. map, bibliog.,
(Monographs of American Ethnological Society,
No.10).

Describes the effect of Islam upon the religious beliefs and practices of the pagan Hausa
(Maguzawa) of Kano.

714.   ------,

''Islam and clan organization among the Hausa.''
Southwestern Journal of Anthropology, v.3, 1947:
p.193-211.

715.   ------,

''Some aspects of Negro Mohammedan culture
contact among the Hausa.'' American Anthropolo-
gist, v.43, No.1, January-March, 1941: p.51-61.

716. GUEYE, Djime Momar

''Les trois objectifs et les qutre caractères de la lutte de El Hadj Cheikh Oumar Tall, heros musulman de notre resistance nationale.'' Vers l'Islam, (Dakar) May-June 1965: p.7-10.

717. HALLUM, W.K.R.

''The Bayajida legend in Hausa folklore.'' Journal of African History, v.7, No.1, 1966: p.47-60.

718. HAMA, Boubou

Histoire des Songhay. Paris, Padoux, 1964.

719. HASSAN, Alhaji and NA'IBI, Mallam Shuaibu

A chronicle of Abuja. Translated and arranged from the Hausa of Alhaji Hassan and Mallam Shuaibu Na'ibi by Frank Heath. Ibadan, Ibadan University Press, 1952. 91p.

720. HISKETT, M.

''The Arab star-calendar and planetary system in Hausa verse.'' Bulletin of the School of Oriental and African Studies, v.30, No.1, 1967: p.158-176.

721. ------,

''The development of Islam in Hausaland.'' In Northern Africa: Islam and modernisation, papers on the theme of Islamisation, modernisation, nationalism and independence presented and discussed at a symposium arranged by the African Studies Association of the United Kingdom on the occasion of its Annual General Meeting, 14 September 1971.

721.   HISKETT, Mervyn (Contd.)

Edited with an introduction by Michael Brett.
London, Cass, 1973: p.57-64.

722.   ------,

''The historical background to the naturalization
of Arabic loan-words in Hausa.'' African Language
Studies, v.6, 1965: p.18-26.

723.   ------,

''Islamic education in the traditional and state
systems in Northern Nigeria.'' In Geoffrey N.
Brown and Mervyn Hiskett. Conflict and harmony
in education in tropical Africa. London, Allen
& Unwin, 1975: p.134-151.

Attempts to describe traditional Islamic
education as it is practiced in Northern Nigeria,
for those who are not already familiar with it.

724.   ------,

''An Islamic tradition of reform in the Western
Sudan from the 16th to the 18th century.''
Bulletin of the School of Oriental and African
Studies, v.25, No.3, 1962: p.588-591.

A discussion based on three unedited works
of Uthman Dan Fodio.

725.   ------,

''Kitab al-Farq: a work on the Habe Kingdoms,
attributed to Uthman Dan Fodio.'' Bulletin of the
School of Oriental and African Studies, v.23,
1960: p.558-579.

726. HISKETT, M.

''Some historical and Islamic influences in
Hausa folklore.'' Journal of the Folklore
Institute, v.4, No.2/3, 1967: p.145-162.

727. ------,

''The state of learning among the Fulani before
the jihad.'' Bulletin of the School of Oriental
and African Studies, v.19, 1957: p.551-599.

728. ------,

Tazyin al-Waraqat, by Abdullah ibn Muhamad.
Ibadan, Ibadan University Press, 1963. 144p.

729. HODGKIN, Thomas L.

Nigerian perspectives: an historical anthology.
London, Oxford University Press, 1960. 340p.
(West African History series).

A collection of passages bearing on the
history of Nigeria before 1900. It is intended
as an anthology rather than a sourcebook.
Contains ten passages on various aspects of
Islam in Nigeria.

730. ------,

''Uthman Dan Fodio.'' Nigeria Magazine. October
1960: p.75-82.

731. HOGBEN, S.J.

An introduction to the history of the Islamic
states of Northern Nigeria. Based on The emirates
of Northern Nigeria, by S.J. Hogben and A.H.M.
Kirk-Greene. Ibadan, Oxford University Press,

731. HOGBEN, S.J. (Contd.)

1967. xvi, 351p.

732. ------,

The Muhammadan emirates of Nigeria. London,
Humphrey Milford, 1929. xiv, 203p.

733. HOGBEN, S.J. and KIRK-GREENE, A.H.M.

The emirates of Northern Nigeria: a preliminary
survey of their historical traditions. London,
Oxford University Press, 1966. 638p. illus.,
bibliog.

734. HOUDAS, O.

''Protestations des habitants de Kano contre les
attaques du Sultan Mohammed-Bello, Roi du Sokoto.''
Homenaje à D. Francisco Codera. Zaragoza, Mariano
Escar, 1904.

735. HUBBARD, J.P.

''Government and Islamic education in Northern
Nigeria (1900-1940).'' In Geoffrey N. Brown and
Mervyn Hiskett. Conflict and harmony in education
in tropical Africa. London, Allen & Unwin, 1975:
p.152-167.

736. HULL, Richard W.

''The impact of the Fulani jihad on interstate
relations in the Central Sudan Katsina emirate:
a case study.'' In McCall, D.F. (and others)
eds. Aspects of West African Islam. Boston,
1971: p.87-100.

737. HUNWICK, J.O.

      ''Islam in Medieval Songhay.'' Unpublished
      Ph.D. dissertation, Department of History,
      University of Ibadan, 1968.

738. ------,

      ''The nineteenth century jihads.'' In Thousand
      years of West African history, edited by J.F.A.
      Ajayi and I. Espie, Camden, N.J. Nelson, 1967:
      p.262-283.

739. ------,

      ''Religion and state in the Songhay empire
      1464-1591.'' In Islam in Tropical Africa, edited
      by I.M. Lewis, London, Oxford University Press,
      1966: p.296-317.

740. ------,

      ''Studies in the Tarikh al Fattash: its authors
      and textual history.'' Research Bulletin (Centre
      of Arabic Documentation, University of Ibadan),
      v.5, Nos. 1&2, December 1969: p.57-65.

741. HUNWICK, J.O. and GWARZO, H.I.
      ''Another look at the De Gironcourt Papers.''
      Research Bulletin (Centre of Arabic Documentation,
      Ibadan), v.3, No.2, 1967: p.74-99.

742. IBN FARTUA, Ahmed
      History of the first twelve years of the reign
      of Mai Idris Alooma of Bornu (1571-1583) by his
      Imam, together with the ''Diwan of the Sultans of
      Bornu'' and ''Girgam'' of the Magumi. Translated

742.   IBN FARTUA, Ahmed (Contd.)

from the Arabic with an introduction and notes
by H.R. Palmer. London, Frank Cass, 1970. 121p.
(Cass library of African Studies. General Studies
no.92).

743.   IFEMESIA, C.C.
''Bornu under the Shehus.'' In J.F.A. Ajayi and
I. Espie. A thousand years of West African
history. Ibadan, Ibadan University Press, 1965:

p.284-293.

744.   IJAODOLA, J.O.
''The proper place of Islamic law in Nigeria.''
Nigeria Law Journal (Lagos), v.3, 1969: p.129-140.

745.   JOHNSTON, H.A.S.
The Fulani empire of Sokoto. London, Oxford
University Press, 1967. xvi, 312p. illus., bibliog.

746.   KANO CHRONICLE
''Muslim missionaries in Kano.'' In Thomas
Hodgkin, Nigerian perspectives: an historical
anthology. London, Oxford University Press,
1960: p.75-76.

747.   LACROIX, P.F.
''L'Islam Peul de l'Adamawa.'' In Islam in
Tropical Africa, edited by I.M. Lewis. London,
Oxford University Press, 1966: p.401-407.

748.   LA RONCIER, Ch. de.
       ''Une histoire du Bornou au xviie siècle.''
       Revue de l'Histoire de Colonies Francaises, v.7,
       No.2, 1919: p.73-88.

749.   LAST, Murray
       ''An aspect of the Caliph Bello's social policy.''
       Kano Studies, No.2, July 1966: p.56-59.

750.   ------,
       ''Reform in West Africa: the jihad movements of
       the nineteenth century.'' In The History of
       West Africa, vol.2, edited by J.F.A. Ajayi and
       Michael Crowder. London, Longman, 1974: p.1-29.

751.   ------,
       ''A note on attitudes to the supernatural in the
       Sokoto jihad.'' Journal of the Historical Society
       of Nigeria, v.4, No.1, December 1967: p.3-13.

752.   ------,
       The Sokoto Caliphate. London, Longmans, 1967.
       lxxxiii, 280p. illus., bibliog. (Ibadan history
       series).
           An account, based largely on nineteenth-century
       Arabic documents from Sokoto, of the origins and
       history of the Caliphate until the coming of the
       British in 1903. It includes the role of the
       vizierate in maintaining the administrative and
       the spiritual position of the caliphate.

753. LAST, Murray
    ''A solution to the problems of dynastic chrono-
    logy in nineteenth century Zaria and Kano.''
    Journal of the Historical Society of Nigeria,
    v.3, No.3, 1966.

754. LAST, Murray and AL-HAJJ, M.A.
    ''Attempts at defining a Muslim in nineteenth
    century Hausaland and Bornu.'' Journal of the
    Historical Society of Nigeria, v.3, No.2,
    December 1965: p.231-241.

755. LAVERS, John E.
    ''Islam in the Bornu caliphate: a survey.''
    Odu; New series, No.5, April 1971: p.27-53.
        Attempts a survey of some aspects of Islam
    in Bornu in the period 1500-1800.

756. ------,
    ''Jibril Gaini: a preliminary account of the
    career of a Mahdist leader in North-Eastern
    Nigeria.'' Research Bulletin (Centre of Arabic
    Documentation, University of Ibadan), v.3, No.1,
    January 1967: p.16-39.

757. LOVEJOY, Paul E.
    Long distance trade and Islam: the case of the
    Nineteenth Century Hausa Kola trade. (Paper
    presented at the Thirteenth Annual Meeting of the
    African Studies Association. Boston, October 21-24
    1970). 16p. Bibliography.

758. LOW, V.N.
    ''The border emirates: a political history of
    three north-east Nigerian emirates c.1800-1902.''
    Ph.D. Thesis, U.C.L.A. 1968.

759. MACINTYRE, J.L.
    ''Islam in Northern Nigeria.'' Moslem World,
    V.2, April 1912: p.144-151.

760. MAHRAM OF UMME JILMI
    ''Kanem: the coming of Islam.'' In Thomas
    Hodgkin, Nigerian perspectives: an historical
    anthology. London, Oxford University Press,
    1960: p.68-69.

761. MARTIN, B.G.
    ''Kanem, Bornu and the Fazzan: notes on the
    political history of a trade route.'' Journal
    of African History, v.10, No.1, 1969: p.15-27.

762. ------,
    A muslim political tract from Northern Nigeria.
    Muhammed Bello's Usul al-Siyasa. In McCall,
    D.F. (and others) (eds). Aspects of West African
    Islam. Boston, 1971: p.63-86. illus.

763. ------,
    ''A new Arabic history of Ilorin.'' Research
    Bulletin (Centre of Arabic Documentation, Ibadan),
    v.1, No.2, 1965: p.20-27.

764. el-MASRI, F.H.
        ''Islam.'' In Lloyd, P.C. (and others). The
        City of Ibadan... London, 1967: p.249-257.

765. ------,
        ''Islam in Ibadan.'' In The city of Ibadan,
        edited by P.C. Lloyd, A.L. Mabogunje & B. Awe.
        London, Cambridge University Press in association
        with the Institute of African Studies, University
        of Ibadan, 1967: p.249-257.

766. ------,
        ''The life of Shehu Usuman Dan Fodio before the
        jihad.'' Journal of the Historical Society of
        Nigeria, v.2, No.4, 1963: p.435-448.

767. el-MASRI, F.H. and others.
        ''Sifofin Shehu: an autobiography and character
        study of 'Uthman b. Fudi in verse.'' Research
        Bulletin (Centre for Arabic Documentation,
        Ibadan), v.2, No.1, January 1966: p.1-36.

768. MBAYE, El-Hadji Ravane
        ''Un apercu de l'Islam Songhay, ou reponses d'
        Al-Magili aux questions posées par Askia El-Hadj
        Muhammad, Empereur de Gao.'' Bulletin de l'Instit
        Fondamental d'Afrique Noire, serie B, v.34, No.2,
        April 1972: p.237-267.

769. MEANS, J.E.
        ''A study of the influence of Islam in Northern
        Nigeria.'' Ph.D. Thesis, Georgetown University,
        1965.

770. MORTON-WILLIAMS, Peter
''The Fulani penetration into Nupe and Yoruba in the nineteenth century.'' In History and social anthropology, edited by I.M. Lewis, London, Tavistock, 1968: p.1-24, bibliog.

771. MUHAMMAD, Abd Allah Ibn
''The Hijra and holy war of Sheik Uthman Dan Fodio.'' In Robert O. Collins, (ed.). African history: text and readings. New York, Random House, 1971: p.59-67.

Abd Allah Ibn Muhammad was the younger brother of Sheik Uthman Dan Fodio. He served as his brother's wazir after the declaration of holy war against Yunfa, the Sarki of Gobir. Abd Allah recorded the hijra and the jihad in prose and verse in his Tazyin al-Waraqat.

772. MUHAMMAD, Yahaya
''The legal status of Muslim women in the northern states of Nigeria.'' Journal. Centre for Islamic Legal Studies, (Zaria), v.1, No.2, 1967: p.1-38.

773. NADEL, S.F.
Nupe religion: traditional beliefs and the influence of Islam in a West African chiefdom. New York, Schocken Books, 1970. 288p.

A scholarly and penetrating study of Nupe religion and worship showing the influence of Islam on the traditional religious beliefs of the people.

774. NJEUMA, Martin Z.
''Adamawa and Mahdism: the career of Hayatu Ibn
Sa'id in Adamawa, 1878-1898.'' Journal of African
History, v.12, No.1, 1971: p.61-77.

775. ------,
The rise and fall of Fulani rule in Adamawa,
1809-1901. London, School of Oriental and
African Studies, 1969.

776. NORTHERN NIGERIA. History Research Scheme
First interim report. Zaria, 1966.
Contains lists of Arabic manuscripts held
on microfilm at Ahmadu Bello University, Zaria.

777. OGUNBIYI, I.A.
''The position of Muslim women as stated by
c Uṭhman b. Fudi.'' Odu, v.2, October 1969:
p.43-60. bibliog.

778. ONYIOHA, K.O.K.
Christianity, Islam and Godianism in Nigeria.
Enugu, the Author, 1964. 15p. illus.
A lecture delivered at the University
of Nigeria, Nsukka.

779. ORR, Sir Charles
The making of Northern Nigeria. With a new
introduction by A.H.M. Kirk-Greene. London,
Frank Cass, 1965. 306p.

780. OSUNTOKUN, Jide
''The response of the British colonial government

780. OSUNTOKUN, Jide (Cɒntd.)

in Nigeria to Islamic insurgency in the French
Sudan and the Sahara during the first world
war.'' Bulletin de l'Institut Fondamental d'
Afrique Noire, v.36, serie B, No.1, 1974:
p.15-24.

781. OTTENBERG, Simon
''A Moslem Igbo village.'' Cahiers d'Etudes
Africaines, v.11, No.2, 1971: p.231-260. bibliog.

782. PADEN, John Naber
''The influence of religious elites on political
culture and community integration in Kano,
Nigeria.'' Ph.D. Thesis, Harvard University, 1968.

783. PALMER, Sir Herbert Richmond
The Bornu, Sahara and Sudan. London, John
Murray, 1936.

784. ------,
''An early Fulani conception of Islam (translation
of Tanbihu l'Ikhwan, attributed to Shehu Dan
Fodio).'' Journal of African Society, v.13, No.52,
July 1914: p.407-414; v.14, No.53, October 1914:
p.53-59.

785. ------,
''The Kano chronicle.'' Journal of the Anthropological Institute, v.38, 1909: p.58-98.

786.   PALMER, Herbert Richmond
       ''A Muslim divine of the Sudan in fifteenth
       century.''   Africa, v.3, No.2, April 1930:
       p.203-216.
            A commentary on the time and reign of Gaji
       Dunamanii, the sultan of Bornu who is believed
       to have ruled from 1472-1504.

'87.   PARRINDER, E.G.
       ''Moslem revival in Nigeria.''   West Africa,
       30 July 1955: p.498.

788.   QUINN, Charlotte A.
       ''A nineteenth-century Fulbe state.''   Journal
       of African History, v.12, 1971: p.427-440.

789.   RATO, Bernabe
       ''Los Hausas y su Islam (The Hausa and Islam).''
       Africa, (Madrid), v.23, No.297, September 1966:
       p.15-19. illus.
            An outline of some aspects of Hausa life
       today and its Islamic background, with references
       to the development of Hausa studies.

790.   RODD, Francis
       ''A Fezzani military expedition to Kanem and
       Bagirmi in 1821.''   Journal of the Royal African
       Society, v.35, 1936: p.153-168.

791.   ROUCH, Jean
       Contribution à l'histoire des Songhay.   Memoire,
       Institut Fondamental d'Afrique Noire, No.29,

791. ROUCH, Jean (Contd.)

        1953: p.137-250.

792. RUBIN, Arnold
        Problems for Islamic influence in the Benue
        borderland. ASAP, 1967. 19p.

793. SADLER, George W.
        ''Mohammedanism in Nigeria.'' Moslem World,
        v.35, No.2, April 1945: p.135-137.

794. SAINTE-CROIX, F.W. de.
        The Fulani of Northern Nigeria. Lagos, Government
        Printer, 1945.

795. SAINT-MARTIN, Y.
        ''L'artillerie d'El Hadj Omar et d'Ahmadou.''
        Bulletin de l'Institut Fondamental d'Afrique
        Noire, Series B, v.27, 1967.

796. ------,
        ''La volonté de paix d'El Hadj Omar et d'Ahmadou
        dans leurs relations avec la France.'' Bulletin
        de l'Institut Fondamental d'Afrique Noire, v.30,
        series B, No.3, 1968: p.785-802.

797. SALIH, Muhammad
        ''Umar ibn Uthman at N'gazargamu.'' In Thomas
        Hodgkin, Nigerian perspectives: an historical
        anthology. London, Oxford University Press,
        1960: p.134-135.

798. SAMB, Amar

Sur El Hadj Omar (à propos d'un article d'Yves
Saint-Martin.'' Bulletin de l'Institut Fondamenta
d'Afrique Noire, v.30, series B, No.3, 1968:
p.803-805.

799. ------,

''La vie d'El-Hadji Omar par Cheikh Moussa Kamara.
Bulletin de l'Institut Fondamental d'Afrique Noire
v.32, series B, No.1, 1970: p.44-135; No.3, 1970:
p.770-818.

800. SCHULTZE, Arnold

The Sultanate of Bornu, translated from the
German by P.A. Benton. London, Oxford University
Press, 1914. 401p.

801. SHANI, Ma'aji Isa

''The status of Muslim women in the northern
states of Nigeria.'' Journal. Centre for Islamic
Legal Studies (Zaria), v.1, No.2, 1967: p.39-52.

802. SMITH, H.F.C.

''The death of Shehu Muhammad al-Aminu al-Kanemi.'
Bulletin of News, Historical Society of Nigeria,
v.6, No.2, September 1961.

803. ------,

''The dynastic chronology of Fulani Zaria.''
Journal of the Historical Society of Nigeria,
v.2, No.2, 1961: p.277-285.

804.   SMITH, H.F.C.   (Contd.)

''A forgotten Hausa historian of Timbuktu?.''
Bulletin of News, Historical Society of Nigeria,
v.4, No.1, June 1959.

805.   ------,

''A fragment of 18th century Katsina and A further
adventure in the chronology of Katsina.'' Bulletin of the Nigerian Historical Society, v.4,
No.4, and v.6, No.1, 1961.

806.   ------,

''A further adventure in the chronology of
Katsina.'' Bulletin of News, Historical Society
of Nigeria, v.1, No.1, June 1961.

807.   ------,

''The Islamic revolution of the 19th century.''
Journal of the Historical Society of Nigeria,
v.2, No.2, 1961.

808.   ------,

''Muhammad Bello Amir al-mu'minin.'' Ibadan,
v.10, June 1960: p.16-19.

809.   ------,

''A neglected theme of West African history: the
Islamic revolutions of the 19th century.''
Journal of the Historical Society of Nigeria,
v.2, No.2, December 1961: p.169-185.

810.   ------,

''A note on Muhammad al-Maghili.'' Bulletin of

810. SMITH, H.F.C. (Contd.)

    News, Historical Society of Nigeria, v.7, No.3,
    December 1962.

811. ------,

    ''A seventeenth century writer of Katsina.''
    Bulletin of News, Historical Society of Nigeria,
    v.6, No.1, 1961. supplement.

812. ------,

    ''The Wazir Abd al-Qadir Ibn Uthman of Sokoto.''
    Bulletin of News, Historical Society of Nigeria,
    v.4, No.3, 1959.

813. SMITH, H.F.C., D.M. LAST and G. GUBIO
    ''Ali Eisami Gazirmabe of Bornu.'' In Africa
    remembered, edited by Philip Curtin. Madison,
    University of Wisconsin Press, 1967: p.199-216.

814. SMITH, M.G.
    ''A Hausa kingdom: Maradi under Dan Baskore,
    1854-75.'' In West African Kingdoms in the
    Nineteenth Century, ed. by D. Forde and P.M.
    Kaberry. London, Oxford University Press for the
    International African Institute, 1967: p.93-122.

815. ------,

    ''The Jihad of Shehu Dan Fodio: some problems.''
    In Islam in Tropical Africa, edited by I.M. Lewis.
    London, Oxford University Press, 1966: p.408-424.

816. STENNING, D.J.

''Cattle values and Islamic values in a pastoral
population.'' In Islam in Tropical Africa, edited
by I.M. Lewis. London, Oxford University Press,
1966: p.387-400.

This paper is about the place of Islamic
observance in the ceremonial and ritual life of
the Wodaabe pastoral Fulani of Bornu in Northern
Nigeria.

817. TAPIERO, Norbert

''Le grand Shaykh Peul Uthman Ibn Fudi (Othman
Dan Fodio, mort en 1232 H-1816 J.C.) et certaines
sources de son Islam doctrinal.'' Revues des
Etudes Islamiques, v.31, No.1, 1963: p.49-88.

818. TEMPLE, O. and TEMPLE, C.L. (eds.)

Notes on the tribes, provinces, emirates, and
states of the Northern Provinces of Nigeria.
Lagos, Church Missionary Society, 1922.

819. TOMLINSON, G.J.F. and LETHEM, G.J.

History of Islamic propaganda in Nigeria. London,
Waterlow, (n.d.)

820. TUKUR, Bashiru

''Koranic schools in Northern Nigeria.'' West
African Journal of Education, v.7, October 1963:
p.149-152.

Emphasis on teaching in Koranic schools is
on memorization, not understanding. The value
of their education is that the pupils acquire
some knowledge of Arabic in addition to becoming

147

820. TUKUR, Bashiru (Contd.)

      literate in 'El Ajami.'

821. TYAM, Mohammadon Alion
      ''The life of Al-Hajj Umar.'' In Robert O.
      Collins, (ed). African history: text and readings.
      New York, Random House, 1971: p.98-110.
        The life of Al-Hajj Umar is a long eulogistic
      poem written in Fulani by one of Sheik Umar's
      earliest disciples (having joined him in 1864).
      The author was one of the Sheik's most loyal
      followers.

822. ------,
      La vie d'el Hadj Omar. Trad. par H. Gaden.
      Paris, Institut d'Ethnologie, 1935. (Memoires
      de l'Institut d'Ethnologie, no.21).

823. URVOV, Yves
      ''Chronologie du Bornu.'' Journal de la Société
      des Africanistes, v.11, 1941: p.21-32: v.12,
      No.2, 1942: p.271-289.

824. ------,
      Histoire de l'empire du Bornu. Paris, Librairie
      Larose, 1949. 166p. (Memoires de l'Institut
      Francais d'Afrique Noire, no.7).

825. VERMEL, Pierre
      ''L'influence du mahdisme au Nigeria.'' Afrique
      et Asie, v.93/94, 1971: p.47-60. Bibliog.

826. VICARS-BOYLE, C.
"Historical notes on the Yola Fulani."
Journal of the African Society, v.10, No.27,
1910.

827. WALDMAN, Marilyn Robinson
"The Fulani jihad: a reassessment." Journal
of African History, v.6, No.3, 1965: p.333-355.

828. ------,
"A note on the ethnic interpretation of the
Fulani jihad." Africa, v.36, No.3, July 1966:
p.286-291.

829. WILKS, Ivor and FERGUSON, Phyllis.
"In vindication of Sidi al—Hajj Abd al—Salam
Shabayni." In Allen, Christopher and Johnson,
R.W. (eds). African perspectives: papers in the
history, politics and economics of Africa,
presented to Thomas Hodgkin. Cambridge, University Press, 1970: p.35-52. illus.

830. YELD, E.R.
"Islam and social stratification in Northern
Nigeria." British Journal of Sociology, v.11,
No.2, June 1960: p.112-128.
      Social stratification in the Fulani dominated
Hausa emirates of Nigeria is examined in an attempt
to show that factors operating to determine status
among the people concerned are applicable through-
out the society.

831. YUSUF, Ahmed Beita
      ''Capital formation and management among the
      Muslim Hausa traders of Kano, Nigeria.''
      Africa, v.45, No.2, 1975: p.167-182.

      Attempts to comment on the various techniques
      by which Kano Hausa traders and businessmen raise
      capital and invest it for diverse economic and
      social returns.

SENEGAL

832. ADAM, M.
      ''Legendes historiques du pays Mjoro (Sahel).''
      Revue Coloniale, 1903: pp.81-98, 232-248, 354-372,
      485-896, 602-620, 734-744.

833. ARNAUD, R.
      ''La singuliere legende de Soninke. Traditions
      orales sur le royaume de Koumbi et sur divers
      autres royaumes soudanais.'' In L'Islam et la
      politique francaise. Paris, Comité de l'Afrique
      francaise, 1912: p.144-185.

834. BARRY, Boubacar
      ''La guerre des Marabouts dans la region du
      Fleuve Senegal de 1673 à 1677.'' Bulletin de
      l'Institut Fondamental d'Afrique Noire (Dakar)
      v.33 (B), No.3, July 1971: p.564-589.

835. BATHILY, Abdoulaye
      ''Mamadou Lamine Drame et la resistance anti-
      imperialiste dans le Haut-Senegal, (1885-1888).''

835.   BATHILY, Abdoulaye (Contd.)

Notes Africaines, No.125, January 1970: p.20-31.

836.   BATHILY, I.D.
       ''Notices socio-historiques sur l'ancien royaume
       Soninke du Gadiaga.'' Bulletin de l'Institut
       Fondamental d'Afrique Noire, v.31, 1969: p.31-105.

837.   BECKER, C. and MARTIN, V.
       ''Memoire inedit de Doumet (1769): le Kayor et
       les pays voisins au cours de la deuxieme moitie
       du xviii^e siecle.'' Bulletin de l'Institut
       Fondamental d'Afrique Noire, v.36, serie B, No.1,
       1974: p.25-92.

838.   BEHRMAN, Lucy
       ''French Muslim policy and the Senegalese brother-
       hoods.'' In Aspects of West African Islam, edited
       by D.F. McCall (and others). Boston, African
       Studies Center, Boston University, 1971: p.185-
       208.

839.   ------,
       ''The Islamization of the Wolof by the end of the
       nineteenth century.'' In McCall, Daniel F. (et
       al) (eds). Western African history. New York,
       1969: p.102-131, bibliog.

840.   ------,
       Muslim brotherhoods and politics in Senegal.
       Cambridge, Mass., Harvard University Press, 1970.
       224p.

840.   BEHRMAN, Lucy C. (Contd.)

An inquiry into the political power of the
venerated 'marabus' of the Senegal and their
resistance to certain programs of social change
which might undermine their privileged position
in Senegalese society.

841.   ------,
''The political significance of the Wolof
adherence to Muslim brotherhoods in the nineteenth century.'' African Historical Studies,
v.1, No.1, 1968: p.60-77.

842.   BERGMANN, Herbert
''Les notables villageois: chef de village et
imam face à la cooperative rurale dans une
region du Senegal.'' Bulletin de l'Institut
Fondamental d'Afrique Noire, serie B, v.36, No.2,
April 1974: p.283-322.

843.   BESLIER, Geneviève
Le Senegal: l'Antiquité, les Arabes et les
empires noirs. Paris, Payot, 1935.

844.   BOILAT, P.D.
Esquisses Senegalaises. Paris, Bertrand, 1853.

845.   BOMBA, Victoria
''The pre-nineteenth century political tradition
of the Wolof.'' Bulletin de l'Institut Fondamental d'Afrique Noire, v.36, serie B, No.1, 1974:
p.1-13.

846. BOUCHE, P. and MAUNY, R.
''Sources écrites relatives à l'histoire de Peuls
et des Toucouleurs.'' Notes Africaines, v.31,
No.7, 1946: p.7-9.

847. BOULEGUE, J.
''Contribution à la chronologie du royaume du
Saloum.'' Bulletin de l'Institut Fondamental
d'Afrique Noire, series B, v.28, 1966: p.657-662.

848. BOULEGUE, J. and PINTO-BULL, B.
''Les relations du Cayor avec le Portugal dans
la premiere moitie du xvie siecle, d'après deux
documents nouveaux.'' Bulletin de l'Institut
Fondamental d'Afrique Noire, v.28, series B,
Nos. 3/4, 1966: p.663-667.

849. BOURGEAU, J.
''Notes sur la coutume de Sereres du Saloum.''
Bulletin du comité d'Etudes Historiques et
Scientifiques de l'Afrique Occidentale francaise,
v.16, 1933: p.1-65.

850. BOURLON, Abel
''Actualité des Mourides et du mouridisme.''
Afrique et Asie, v.46, 1959: p.10-30.
An account of the Mourid brotherhood numbe-
ring over 400,000 Wolofs which is about a quarter
of the Muslim population in the Senegal.

851. ------,
''L'evolution politique du Senegal 1962-1964.''
L'Afrique et L'Asie, No.68, 1964: p.23-41.

852. BOURLON, Abel
''Mourides et mouridisme 1953.'' In Notes et etudes sur l'Islam en Afrique Noire. Paris, 1962: p.53-74.

853. CHAILLEY, Marcel
''Quelques aspects de l'Islam senegalais.'' Academie des Sciences d'Outre-mer. Comptes rendus, v.22, No.6, p.249-262.

854. CISSOKO, S.M.
''Civilization Wolof-Serere.'' Présence Africaine No.62, 1967: p.121-167.

855. ------,
''Introduction à l'histoire des Mandingues de l'Ouest: l'empire de Kabou (16e - 19e siecle).'' Conference on Manding Studies, School of Oriental and African Studies, London, 1972. unpublished.

856. COIFMAN, V.
''History of the Wolof state of Jolof until 1860. Including comparative data from the Wolof state of Walo.'' Unpublished Dissertation, University of Wisconsin, 1969.

857. COLOMBANI, F.M.
''Extraits d'une monographie du Gudimaka par l'administrateur Colombani.'' In Chroniques du Fouta-Senegalais, edited by M. Delafosse and H. Gaden. Paris, 1913: p.131-136.

858. COPANS, J. et al

Maintenance sociale et changement economique au Senegal. Doctrine economique et pratique du travail chez les Mourides. Paris, Office de Recherche Scientifique et technique. Outre-mer 1972, 274p. illus. (Travaux et documents, ORSTOM, 15).

859. COUTY, Philippe
Doctrine et pratique du travail chez les Mourides. Dakar, Centre ORSTOM, 1968.

860. DELAFOSSE, Maurice
''Les confreries musulmanes et la maraboutisme dans les pays du Senegal et du Niger.'' L'Afrique Francaise, v.21, 1911. p.1.

861. ------,
''Traditions musulmanes relatives à l'origine de Peuls.'' Revue du Monde Musulman, v.20, July/September 1912: p.242-267.

862. DELAFOSSE, Maurice and GADEN, Henri
Chroniques du Fouta senegalais, traduites de deux manuscrits arabes inedits de sire-Abbas-Soh, et accompagnées de notes, documents annexes et commentaires, d'un glossaire et de cartes. Paris, Ernest Leroux, 1913.

863. DIA, A.C.
Les derniers jours de Lat Dior, suivi de la mort du Damel. Paris, Présence Africaine, 1965.

864. DIOP, Amadou-Bamba
          ''Lat Dior et le probleme musulman.'' Bulletin
          de l'Institut Fondamental d'Afrique Noire, v.28,
          (B), Nos. 1/2, January-April, 1966: p.493-539.
              Lat Dior and his relatives, whether by
          sincere conviction or by political opportunism,
          became converted to Islam towards the middle of
          the 18th century.

865. DUMONT, Fernand
          Amadou Bamba, apôtre de la non-violence (1850-1927)
          Notes Africaines IFAN (Dakar), No.121, January
          1969: p.20-24.

866. FISHER, Humphrey J.
          ''The early life and pilgrimage of Al-Hajj
          Muhammad al-Amin the Soninke (d.1887).'' Journal
          of African History, v.11, No.1, 1970: p.51-69.bibl
          iog.

867. GADEN, Henri
          ''Note de M. Gaden a propos du War-Dyabi, War
          Dyabe ou War-Ndyay de Bekri.'' In M. Delafosse
          and H. Gaden. (eds). Chroniques du Fouta Sene-
          galais, Paris, 1913: p.182-185.

868. ------,
          ''Tarikh peul de Douentza (1895).'' Bulletin de
          l'Institut Fondamental d'Afrique Noire, v.30,
          series B, No.2, 1968: p.682-690.

869. GAMBLE, David P.
          The Wolof of Senegambia. London, International

869.   GAMBLE, David P. (Contd.)

        African Institute, 1957.

870.   GANIER, G.

        ''Maures et Toucouleurs, sur les deux rives du
        Senegal. La mission de Victor Ballot aupres de
        Sidi Ely, roi de Maures Braknas fevrier-juin
        1884.'' Bulletin de l'Institut Fondamental d'
        Afrique Noire, v.30, series B, No.1, 1968: p.182-
        226.

871.   GOUILLY, A.

        ''Les mosquées du Senegal.'' Revue Juridique et
        Politique, No.4, October-December, 1965. p.531-
        536.

872.   HALPERN, Jan

        ''La confrerie des Mourides et le developpement
        au Senegal.'' Cultures et Developpement (Louvain),
        v.4, No.1, 1972: p.99-125.

873.   HARGREAVES, J.D.

        ''The Tokolor empire of Segou and its relations
        with the French.'' Boston University Papers on
        African History, v.2, 1966.

874.   HOLAS, Bohumil

        ''La chef des songes des Musulmans Senegalais.''
        Notes Afrique IFAN, v.42, April 1949: p.45-49.

875.   HOLDERER, P.

        ''Note sur la coutume Mandingue du Ouli.'' In

875. HOLDERER, P. (Contd.)

Coutumiers juridiques de l'Afrique occidentale
francaise. Vol.1, Senegal, Paris, Larose, 1939.

876. HUNWICK, John
''Notes on a late fifteenth-century document
concerning al-Takrur.'' In Allen, Christopher
and Johnson, R.W. (eds). African perspectives:
papers in the history, politics and economics
of Africa, presented to Thomas Hodgkin.
Cambridge, University Press, 1970: p.7-33.

877. HURE, C.
''L'Islam et les droits de la femme en Algerie
et au Senegal.'' Paris, Institut de Droit Comparé,
(n.d.).

878. KESBY, J.D.
''Islam in Senegal.'' Islamic Quarterly, v.7,
1963: p.40-50.

879. KLEIN, Martin A.
Islam and imperialism in Senegal: Sine-Saloum,
1847-1914. Stanford, Calif., Published for the
Hoover Institution by Stanford University Press.
1968. 285p. bibliog.

880. ------,
''The Moslem revolution in nineteenth-century
Senegambia.'' In McCall, Daniel F. et al (eds).
Western African history. New York, 1969:
p.69-101.

SENEGAL

881. KLEIN, Martin A.

Process of Islamization in late 19th century
Senegambia. Berkeley, Department of History,
University of California, 1967. 27p.

882. LEVTZION, Nehemia
The differential impact of Islam among the
Soninke and the Manding. Conference on Manding
Studies. London, School of Oriental and African
Studies, 1927. 21p.

883. MARGOLIOUTH, D.S.
''Contribution to the biography of Abd-al-Qadir.''
Journal of the Royal Asiatic Society, 1907:
p.267-310.

884. MARKOVITZ, Irving L.
''Traditional social structure: the Islamic
brotherhoods and political development in
Senegal.'' Journal of Modern African Studies,
v.8, No.1, April 1970: p.73-96.

885. MARONE, Ibrahima
''Le Tidjanisme au Senegal.'' Bulletin de l'
Institut Fondamental d'Afrique Noire, v.32,
Series B, No.1, 1970: p.136-215.

886. MARTY, Paul
Etudes sur l'Islam au Senegal. Paris, Leroux,
1917. 2vols. (Revue du monde musulman, 13).

887. ------,
Les Mourides d'Amadou Bamba. Rapport à M. Le

159

887.   MARTY, Paul (Contd.)

Gouverneur de l'Afrique occidentale. Paris,
Leroux, 1913. 167p.

888.   ------,

''Tableau historique de Cheikh Sidia.''
Bulletin, Comité d'Etudes Historiques et Scientifique de l'Afrique Occidentale francaise, 1921:
p.76-95.

889.   MEHMMED ALI AINI

Un grand saint de l'Islam: Abd Al-Kadir Guilani,
Paris, 1938.

890.   MOMBEYA, Tierno Mouhammadou-Samba

Sow, Alfa Ibrahim. Le Filon du bonheur eternel.
Paris, Colin, 1971. 200p. (Classiques africains,
10).

891.   MONTEIL, Vincent

''Le Dyolof et Al-Bouri N'Diaye.'' Bulletin de
l'Institut Fondamental d'Afrique Noire, v.28,
series B, Nos. 3/4, 1966: p.595-635.

892.   ------,

''Une confrerie musulmane: les Mourides du
Senegal.'' Archives de Sociologie des Religions,
v.14, July-December 1962: p.77-102.

893.   ------,

''Islam et developpement au Senegal.''
Cahiers de l'Institut de Science Economique

893. MONTEIL, Vincent (Contd.)

Appliquée (Paris), v.120, 1961: p.43-68.

894. ------,

''Lat-Dyor, Damel du Kayor (1842-1886) et l'
Islamisation des Wolofs du Senegal.'' In
Islam in Tropical Africa, edited by I.M. Lewis,
London, Oxford University Press, 1966: p.343-349.
Also in Archives de Sociologie des Religions,
v.16, July-December 1963: p.77-104.

895. ------,

''Un visionnaire musulman senegalais (1946-1965).''
Archives de Sociologie des Religions, v.19,
January-June 1965: p.69-98.

896. ------,

''The Wolof kingdom of Kayour.'' In West African
Kingdoms in the Nineteenth century, edited by
D. Forde and P.M. Kaberry. London, Oxford
University Press for the International African
Institute, 1967: p.260-281.

897. MOREAU, R.L.

''Les marabouts de Dori.'' Archives de Sociologie
des Religions, v.27, 1964: p.113-134.

898. MOURADIAN, Jacques

''Note sur quelques emprunts de la langue Wolof
à l'arable.'' Bulletin de l'Institut Fondamental
d'Afrique Noire, v.2, No.3/4, 1940: p.269-284.

899. al-NAQAR, Umar
       ''Takrur: the history of a name.'' Journal of
       African History (London), v.10, No.3, 1969:
       p.365-374.

900. NDIAYE, Aissatou
       ''Complements à une note sur les emprunts de la
       langue Wolof à l'Arabe.'' Notes Africaines,
       v.41, 1949: p.26-29.

901. NIANE, D.T.
       ''Koly Tenguella et le Tekrour.'' In Congress
       International des Africanistes. Paris, Presence
       Africaine, 1972: p.61-76.

902. NORRIS, H.T.
       ''The history of Shinqit according to the Idaw-
       Ali tradition.'' Bulletin de l'IFAN, v.24,(B)
       Nos. 3/4, July-October 1962: p.393-413.

903. NOWAK, Bronislav
       ''Rola czarnych Kupcow Diula w islamizacji
       Afryki Zachodniej.'' (The role of black Dyula
       merchants in the Islamization of West Africa).
       Przeglad Historyczny, v.60, No.3, 1969: p.537-553.

904. O'BRIEN, Donal Cruise
       The Mourides of Senegal: the political and
       economic organization of an Islamic brotherhood.
       Oxford, Clarendon Press, 1971: 321p. bibliog.
       (Oxford Studies in African affairs).

905. O'BRIEN, Donal Cruise
''Mouride studies''(review article). Africa,
v.40, No.3, July 1970: p.257-260.

906. ------,
''The Saint and the squire; personalities and
social forces in the development of a religious
brotherhood.'' In African perspectives. ed. by
C. Allen and R.W. Johnson, New York, Cambridge
University Press, 1970: p.157-169.
    Treats the Mouride brotherhood of Senegal
as a case study in social forces giving rise to
religious brotherhoods in West Africa.

907. ------,
''Le talibe mouride: étude d'un cas de dependance
sociale (resume).'' Cahiers d'Etudes Africaines,
(Paris), v.9, No.3, 1969: p.502-507.

908. ------,
''Le talibe mouride: la soumission dans une
confrerie religieuse senegalaise.'' Cahiers
d'Etudes Africaines, v.10, No.4, 1970: p.562-578.

909. OLORUNTIMEHIN, B. Olatunji
''The idea of Islamic revolution and Tukulor
constitutional evolution.'' Bulletin. IFAN
(Dakar), v.33,(B) No.4, October 1971: p.675-692.

910. ------,
''Resistance movements in the Tukulor empire.''
Cahiers d'Etudes Africaines, v.8, No.29, 1968.

911. OLARUNTIMEHIN, B. Olatunji
      ''The Segu Tukulor empire: 1848-1893.'' Ph.D.
      Thesis, Ibadan University, 1966.

912. QUESNOT, F.
      ''Les cadres maraboutiques de l'Islam senegala-
      is.'' In Notes et etudes sur l'Islam en Afrique
      Noire. Paris, 1962: p.127-195.

913. ------,
      L'evolution du Tidjanisme senegalais depuis 1922.
      Paris, CHEAM, 1958. (Memoire Cheam, no.2865).

914. ROBIN, J.
      ''L'evolution du mariage coutumier chez les
      musulmans du Senegal.'' Africa, v.17, no.3,
      1947.

915. ROCH, J.
      Les mourides du vieux bassin arachidier Senegalais:
      entretiens recueillis dans la region du Baol.
      Dakar-Hann. Centre ORSTOM, 1971. 113p.

916. ROUSSEAU, R.
      ''Le Senegal d'autrefois: etude sur le Cayor.''
      Bulletin du Comité d'Etudes Historiques et
      Scientifiques de l'Afrique Occidentale Francaise,
      1933: p.237-298.

917. ------,
      ''Le Senegal d'autrefois: étude sur le Qualo.
      Cahiers de Yoro Dara.'' Bulletin du Comité d'

917. ROUSSEAU, R. (Contd.)

Etudes Historiques et Scientifiques de l'Afrique
Occidentale Francaise, 1929: p.133-211.

918. ------,

''Le Senegal d'autrefois: etude sur le Toube.
Papiers de Rawane Boy.'' Bulletin du Comite
d'Etudes Historiques et Scientifiques d'Afrique
Occidentale Francaise, v.15, 1931: p.334-364.

919. ------,

''Le Senegal d'autrefois: seconde étude sur le
Cayor, (complements tirés des manuscrits de
Yoro Dyao).'' Bulletin de l'Institut Fondamen-
tal d'Afrique Noire, v.3, 1941: p.79-144.

920. SAINT-MARTIN, Yves-J.

L'empire toucouleur, 1848-1897. Paris, Le Livre
Africain, 1970. 192p.

History of the spread of Islam into the
Toucoulor empire, Senegal, Mali, Upper Volta,
and the resistance to colonial penetration.

921. ------,

L'empire toucouleur et la France: un demi-siècle
de relations diplomatiques (1846-1893). Dakar,
1967. 482p. (Université de Dakar, Section d'
Histore, publications no.11).

922. ------,

''Les relations diplomatique entre la France
et l'empire toucouleur de 1860 à 1887.''

SENEGAL

922. SAINT-MARTIN, Yves-J (Contd.)

Bulletin de l'Institut Fondamental d'Afrique
Noire, series B, v.27, 1965.

923. SAMB, Amar
''L'education islamique au Senegal.'' Notes
Africaines, (IFAN). No.136, October 1972: p.97-
102.

924. ------,
''Essai sur la contribution du Senegal à la
litterature d'expression arabe.'' Dakar, IFAN,
1972. (Memoire, no.87).

925. ------,
''Influence de l'Islam sur la litterature Wolof.''
Bulletin de l'Institut Fondamental d'Afrique
Noire, v.30, series B, No.2, April 1968: p.628-
641.
    This article traces the influence of Islam
on the Wolof system of thought, language and
literature.

926. ------,
''L'Islam et l'histoire du Senegal.'' Bulletin
de l'IFAN (Dakar), v.33, (B) No.3, July 1971:
p.461-507. bibliog.

927. ------,
''Touba et son Magal.'' Bulletin de l'Institut
Fondamental d'Afrique Noire, v.31 (B), No.3,
July 1969: p.733-753. illus.

928.   SOH, Sire Abbas
       ''Abd al—Qadir in Senegalese Futa.'' In Robert
       O. Collins (ed). African history: text and
       readings. New York, Random House, 1971: p.53-
       58.
            Abd al—Qadir was born in Futa Toro about 1728.
       He established his authority throughout Futa Toro
       by assigning fiefs to his followers during the
       jihad in return for their defence of Senegalese
       Futa.

929.   SY, Cheikh Tidiana
       ''Ahmadou Bamba et l'islamisation des Wolof.''
       Bulletin de l'Institute Fondamentale d'Afrique
       Noire, B, v.32, No.2, 1970: p.412-433.

930.   ——————,
       La confrerie senegalaise des Mourides: un essai
       sur l'Islam au Senegal. Paris, Présence
       africaine. 1969. 354p. illus. Bibliog.

931.   SYLLA, Assane
       ''Les persecutions de Seydina Mouhamadou Limamou
       Laye par les autorités coloniales.'' Bulletin
       de l'IFAN, v.33 (B), No.3, July 1971: p.590-641.

932.   TAUTAIN, L.
       ''Legendes et traditions des Soninke relatives
       à l'empire de Ghanata.'' Bulletin de Geographie
       Historique et Descriptive. 1895: p.472-480.

933.   VILLENEUVE, M.
       ''Une société musulmane d'Afrique noire: la

SENEGAL

933.   VILLENEUVE, M. (Contd.)

confrerie des Mourides.'' Institut des Belles-
lettres Arabes (Tunis), v.28, No.110, 1965:
p.127-216.

934.   WADE, Amadou
''Chronique du Walo senegalais (1186?-1855).:'
Bulletin de l'Institut Fondamental d'Afrique
Noire, v.26, 1964, serie B: p.440-498.

935.   WADE, Abdoulaye
''La doctrine economique du mouridisme.''
Annales Africaines (Dakar), 1967. p.175-206.

936.   WELSH, Isabel Marcus
Islam in Senegal: a study of the Islamic bro-
therhood. M.A. Thesis, University of California,
Berkley, 1965. 59p.

SIERRA LEONE

937.   ABDUL KARIM GHAZALI
''Sierra Leone Muslims and African rituals.''
Sierra Leone Bulletin of Religion, v.2, No.1,
June 1960: p.27-32.

938.   AL-HARAZIM, S.D.
''The origin and progress of Islam in Sierra
Leone.'' Sierra Leone Studies, Old series,
No.21, 1939: p.12-26.

939. ANDERSON, Christian E.
    ''Early muslim schools and British policy in
    Sierra Leone.'' West African Journal of Educa-
    tion.
        Historical account of the rapid growth of
    Islam in Sierra Leone from the 1890s to 1924.

940. FASHOLE-LUKE, Edward W.
    ''Christianity and Islam in Freetown.'' Sierra
    Leone Bulletin of Religion, v.9, No.1, June 1967:
    p.1-16.
        Examines different forms and manifestations
    of the Islamic and Christian religions in con-
    temporary Freetown.

941. ------,
    ''Religion in Freetown.'' In C. Fyfe and E. Jones
    (eds). Freetown; a symposium. Freetown, Sierra
    Leone University Press, 1968: p.127-142.

942. FISHER, Humphrey
    ''Ahmadiyya in Sierra Leone.'' Sierra Leone
    Bulletin of Religion, v.2, 1960: p.1-10. Also
    in West Africa, No.2329, January 1962. p.73.

943. ------,
    ''The modernisation of Islamic education in
    Sierra Leone, Gambia and Liberia: religion and
    language.'' In Geoffrey N. Brown and Mervyn
    Hiskett. Conflict and harmony in education in
    tropical Africa. London, Allen & Unwin, 1975:
    p.187-199.

944.   GHAZALI, Abdul Karim
       ''Sierra Leone Muslims and sacrificial rituals.''
       Sierra Leone Bulletin of Religion, v.2, No.1,
       June 1960: p.27-32.

945.   JUSU, B.M.
       ''The Haidara rebellion of 1931.''   Sierra Leone
       Studies, New series, v.3, December 1954: p.147-153.

946.   KUP, Peter
       ''Islam in Sierra Leone.''   West Africa, No.2214,
       November 1959: p.941, 946.

947.   LITTLE, K.L.
       ''A Moslem missionary in Mendeland, Sierra Leone.'
       Man, v.46, No.102, September-October 1946:
       p.111-113.
           An account of public exhortation by an
       itinerant Moslem priest, illustrating reasons
       for the popularity of Islam in Sierra Leone.

948.   PROUDFOOT, L.
       ''Ahmed Alhadi and the Ahmaddiya in Sierra Leone.'
       Sierra Leone Bulletin of Religion, v.2, No.1,
       June 1960: p.60-68.

949.   ------,
       ''Mosque building and tribal separation in
       Freetown East.''   Africa, v.29, No.4, 1959:
       p.405-416.

950.   PROUDFOOT, L. and WILSON, H.S.
       ''Muslim attitudes to education in Sierra Leone.''

950. PROUDFOOT, L. and WILSON, H.S. (Contd.)

Muslim World, v.50, No.2, 1960: p.86-98.

951. PROUDFOOT, L.
''Towards Muslim solidarity in Freetown.''
Africa, v.31, 1961: p.147-157.

952. SESAY, S.I.
''Koranic schools in the provinces.'' Sierra
Leone Journal of Education, v.1, No.1, April
1966: p.24-26.

Before the advent of Ahmadiyya missionaries
in Sierra Leone, Muslims owed their knowledge
to the pioneering work of Fula and Mandingo
immigrants and traders. Unfortunately however,
the method of Koranic teaching has nothing to
commend itself in the light of modern educational
trends.

953. TRIMINGHAM, J.S. and FYFE, Christopher
''The early expansion of Islam in Sierra Leone.''
Sierra Leone Bulletin of Religion, v.2, No.1,
June 1960: p.33-40.

TOGO

954. DELVAL, R.
''Les musulmans au Togo.'' Afrique et Asie.
No.100, 1974: p.4-21.

955. VOEHRINGER, E.F.
''Meeting Moslems in Togoland.'' Moslem World,
v.31, No.3, July 1941: p.254-262.

956. BERAUD-VILLARS, Jean

L'empire de Gao, un état soudanais aux XVe et XVIe siècles. Paris, Plon, 1942. xxxii, 214p.

957. CARTRY, Michel

''Rapport de mission (religion des Gourmantche).'' Notes et Documentations Voltaiques, (Ougadougou). V.4, No.4, Juil-Septembre, 1971: p.60-66.

958. COLOMBANI, F.M.

''Le Guidimaka: étude geographique, historique et religieuse.'' Bulletin d'Etudes Historiques et Scientifiques de l'Afrique Occidentale Francaise, v.15, 1931: p.365-432.

959. DENIEL, Raymond

Croyances religieuses et vie quotidienne: Islam et Christianisme à Ouagadougou. Paris, Centre National de la Recherche Scientifique. 1970.

360p. (Research voltaique, 14).

960. ECHENBERG, Myron J.

''La'jihad' d'Al-Kari de Bousse, un état marka en pays dafing à la fin du 19e siècle.'' Notes et Documents Voltaiques (Ouagadougou), v.3, No.3, April-June 1970: p.3-42. bibliog.

961. ------,

''Jihad and state building in late nineteenth century Upper Volta: the rise and fall of the Marka state of Al-Kari of Bousse.'' Canadian Journal of African Studies, v.3, No.3, 1969: p.531-561.

962. MAUNY, Raymond
       ''La tour et la mosquée de l'Askia Mohammed à
       Gao.'' Notes Africaines, v.47, 1950: p.66-67.

963. SAUVAGET, J.
       ''Les epitaphes royales de Gao.'' Bulletin de
       l'Institut Fondamental d'Afrique Noire, v.12,
       1950: p.418-440. Also in Al-Andalus, v.15, No.1,
       p.123-141.

964. ------,
       ''Notes preliminaires sur les epitaphes royales
       de Gao.'' Revue des Etudes Islamiques, v.16,
       1948: p.1-12.

965. SKINNER, Elliott P.
       ''Christianity and Islam among the Mossi.''
       American Anthropologist, v.60, No.6, December
       1958: p.1102-1119.

966. ------,
       ''The diffusion of Islam in an African Society.''
       Annals of the New York Academy of Sciences, v.96,
       part 2, January 1962: p.659-669.
          Discusses the factors that led to the spread
       of Islam among the Mossi, inspite of the fact
       that before their conquest by the French the
       Mossi had resisted Islam.

967. ------,
       ''Islam in Mossi society.'' In Islam in Tropical
       Africa, edited by I.M. Lewis. London, Oxford
       University Press, 1966: p.350-373.

UPPER VOLTA

968. VIRE, M.M.
          ''Notes sur trois epitaphes royale de Gao.''
          Bulletin de l'Institut Fondamental d'Afrique
          Noire, v.20, series B, Nos. 3-4, 1958: p.368-376.

CENTRAL AFRICA

969. BECKER, C.H.
          ''Vorbericht uber die islamkundlichen ergenbnisse
          der Innerafrika - expedition des herzogs Adolf
          Friedrich von Mecklenburg.'' Der Islam, v.3,
          1912: p.258-272.

970. COOLEY, William D.
          The negroland of the Arabs examined and explained;
          or, an inquiry into the early history and geogra-
          phy of Central Africa. London, Cass, 1966. 143p.

971. FORGET, D.A.
          L'Islam et le christianisme dans l'Afrique
          centrale. Paris, Librairie Fishbacher, 1900.
          103p.

972. MEINHOF, K.
          ''A plea for missionary work among the Moslems
          of Central Africa.'' Moslem World, April 1911:
          p.155-163.

973. ROOME, W.J.W.
          ''Islam in Equatorial and Southern Africa.''
          Moslem World, July 1914: p.273-290.

CENTRAL AFRICA

974. SHEPPERSON, George
    ''The Jumbe of Kota Kota and some aspects of
    the history of Islam in British Central Africa.''
    In Islam in Tropical Africa, edited by I.M. Lewis.
    London, Oxford University Press, 1966: p.193-207.

CAMEROON

975. MALCOLM, L.W.D.
    ''Islam in the Cameroons.'' Journal of the
    African Society, v.21, 1921: p.35-46.

976. MONTEIL, Charles Victor
    Les Bambara du Segou et du Kaarta. Etude
    historique, ethnographique et litteraire d'une
    peuplade du soudan francais. Paris, Larose,
    1924. 403p.

977. PAGEARD, Robert
    ''Note sur le peuplement du pays de Segou.''
    Journal de la Société des Africanistes, v.31,
    1961: p.83-90.

978. ------,
    Notes sur l'histoire des Bambaras de Segou.
    Clichy, Seine, Edite par l'auteur. 1957. 32p.
    illus.

979. ------,
    ''Une tradition musulman relative à l'histoire
    de Segou. Notes Africaines de l'Institut Fonda-
    mental d'Afrique Noire, v.101, January 1964:
    p.24-26.

CAMEROON

980. PAQUES, Vivian
Les Bambara. Paris, Presses Universitaires de
France, 1954. 123p. illus., bibliog. (Monogra-
phies ethnologiques africaines).

981. ------,
The Bambara. Translated from the French by
Thomas Turner. New Haven, Human Relations Area
Files, 1959. 151p. illus.

982. TAUXIER, L.
Histoire des Bambara. Paris, Geuthner, 1942.
226p.

983. THOMPSON, W.
‘‘Moslem and pagan in Cameroon.’’ Asia, v.24,
October 1924: p.764-767.

CHAD

984. BIOBAKU, Saburu and Al-HAJJ, Muhammad
‘‘The Sudanese Mahdiyya and the Niger-Chad
region.’’ In Islam in Tropical Africa, edited
by I.M. Lewis. London, Oxford University
Press, 1966: p.425-441.

985. CROCQUEVILLE, J.
‘‘Histoire de l’Islamisation du Tchad.’’
Tropiques, v.55, No.393, 1957: p.9-19.

986. HUARD, Paul and BACQUIE, Capt.
‘‘Un établissement islamique dans le desert

986. HUARD, Paul and BACQUIE, Capt. (Contd.)

tchadien: Ouogayi.'' Bulletin de l'Institut
Francais d'Afrique Noire, v.26, 1964: p.1-20.
illus.

987. LEBEUF, J.P. and ROBINSON, M.
''Les mosquées de Fort Lamy (A.E.F.).'' Bulletin
de l'Institut Francais d'Afrique Noire, v.14,
1952: p.970-974.

988. ''NOTES sur les populations musulmanes du territoire
du Tchad, au point de vue politico-religieux.''
Bulletin de la Société de la Recherche Congolaise,
No.4, 1924: p.9-17.

989. ZALTNER, J.C.
''L'installation des Arabes au sud du lac Tchad.''
Abbia, March 1967: p.129-153.

CONGO

990. ABEMBA, J.I.
Pouvoir, politique traditionnel, et Islam au
Congo oriental. Bruxelles, Centre d'Etude et
de Documentation Africaines, 1971. 43p.

991. AJAMI, S.M.
''La société musulmaine et ses regles face à
l'évolution.'' Etudes Congolaises, October-
December 1968.

992. CEULEMANS, P.

''Introduction de l'influence de l'Islam au
Congo.'' In Islam in Tropical Africa, edited
by I.M. Lewis. London, Oxford University Press,
1966: p.174-192.

993. COMHAIRE, Jean

''Notes on the Muslims of Leopoldville.'' (Notes
sur les Musulmans de Leopoldville). Zaire, v.2,
No.3, March 1948: p.303-304.

The Muslim population of Leopoldville is very
stable, and consists of Senegalese and Hausa-
speaking Toucouleur and Hausa respectively.
The former are generally traders and skilled
workers, the latter street traders.

994. HERTOGH, A. de

''Le peril islamique au Congo.'' Bulletin de
la Société Belge d'Etudes, v.17, 1910: p.291-310;
p.713-731.

995. JULIEN, M.

''Mohammed es Senoussi et ses états.'' Bulletin
de la Société des Recherches Congolaises, v.6,
1925: p.104-177.

996. NICKLEWICZ, Piotr.

''Religious and prophetic movements in Congo
and South Africa in the 20th century.'' M.A.
Thesis. Warsaw University, 1965-67.
Written in polish. (unpublished)

997. ROOME, W.J.M.
        ''Islam on the Congo.'' Moslem World, July
        1916: p.282-290.

998. YOUNG, Crawford
        ''L'Islam au Congo.'' Etudes Congolaises, v.10,
        No.5, September-October 1967: p.14-31.
        Even though Islam entered the Congo in the
        19th century with slave-dealers from the coast
        of the Indian Ocean, it encountered Belgian
        resistance and up to 1969 there were only
        300,000 muslims out of a population of 14 million.

NIGER

999. BATRAN, Aziz
        ''Sidi al—Mukhtar al—Kunti and the recrudescence
        of Islam in the Middle Niger Region.'' Ph.D.
        Thesis, University of Birmingham, 1972.

1000. BICHON, B.
        ''Les musulmans de la subdivision de Kombissiry
        (Haute-Volta).'' Notes et etudes sur l'Islam
        en Afrique noire (Recherches et documents du
        CHEAM). V.1, 1962: p.75-102.

1001. BOMBET, A.
        ''Notes sur la situation de l'Islam au Niger.''
        Afrique francais, v.68, No.33, January-February,
        1959: p.4-10.

1002. BOUVAT, L.

''Une collection de manuscrits arabes provenant
des Touareg Oulliminden (Niger).'' Journal
Asiatique, v.209, 1926: p.119-125.

1003. CROWDER, M.

''Islam in Upper Niger.'' Geographical Magazine,
September 1958: p.222-235.

1004. KAUZE

''L'Islam dans le territoire militaire du
Niger.'' Bulletin du Comité d'Etudes Historiques
et Scientifique de l'A.O.F., v.2, April-June
1919: p.177-182.

1005. LAIZE, L.

''L'Islam dans le territoire militaire du Niger.''
Bulletin du Comite d'Etudes Historiques et
Scientifiques de l'A.O.F., 1919: p.177-183.

1006. LEM, F.H.

''Un centre d'Islamisation au moyen-Niger: Say.''
En terre d'Islam (Lyon), v.18, No.22, 1943.

1007. LEROUX, H.

''Animisme et Islam dans la subdivision de
Maradi (Niger).'' Bulletin de l'Institut Francais
d'Afrique Noire, v.10, 1948: p.595-696.

1008. MARTY, Paul

L'Islam et les tribus dans la colonie du Niger
(ex-Zinder). Paris, Geuthner, 1931. Also in:

1008. MARTY, Paul (Contd.)

Revue d'Etudes Islamiques, v.4, 1930: p.333-432.

1009. RAULIN, H.
''Un aspect historique des rapports de l'animisme
et de l'Islam au Niger.'' Journal de la Société
des Africanistes, v.32, No.2, 1962: p.249-274.

1010. TYMOWSKI, M.
''Le Niger, voie de communication des grand
états du Soudan occidental jusqu'a la fin du
xvie siecle.'' Africana Bulletin, No.6, 1967:
p.73-95.

1011. ------,
''La peche à l'époque du moyen âge dans la boucle
du Niger.'' Africana Bulletin, No.12, 1971:
p.7-26.

1012. VAN BERCHEM
''Notes sur les inscriptions arabes estampées
par M. de Gironcourt dans la boucle du Niger.''
Compte-Rendu de l' Academie des Inscriptions et
Belles-Lettres, 1913: p.150-152.

EAST AFRICA (GENERAL)

1013. ABDULLA, Ahmed
''Ambivalence of Muslim education.'' East
African Journal, February 1965, summary in
Oversea Quarterly, v.4, No.7, September 1965:
p.214.

1014.   ADATIA, A.K. and KING, N.Q.
        ''Some East African firmans of H.H. Aga Khan
        III.'' Journal of Religion in Africa, v.2,
        No.3, 1969: p.179-191.

1015.   ALLEN, John
        ''Muslims in East Africa.'' African Ecclessia-
        stical Review, v.7, No.3, July 1965: p.255-262.

1016.   ALPERS, E.A.
        ''Towards a history of the expansion of Islam
        in East Africa: the matrilineal peoples of the
        southen interior.'' In Ranger, T.O. and Kimambo,
        I.N. The historical study of African religion
        with reference to East and Central Africa,
        London, Heinemann, 1972.

1017.   BOURAT, L.
        ''L'Islam dan l'Afrique negre: la civilization
        swahilie.'' Revue du Monde Musulman, v.2, March
        1907: p.10-27.

1018.   CERULLI, Enrico
        ''Islam in East Africa.'' In Religion in the
        Middle East, vol.2, edited by A.J. Arberry.
        New York, Cambridge University Press, 1969.

1019.   CHITTICK, H.N.
        ''Kilwa and the Arab settlement of the East
        African Coast.'' Journal of African History,
        v.4, 1963: p.179-190.

1020. CHITTICK, H.N.

Kisimani Mafia: excavations at an Islamic
settlement on the East African coast. Dar-es-
Salaam, Gov't. Printer, 1961. 33p. (Ministry of
Education. Antiquities Division. Occasional
paper.1).

1021. DAMANN, Ernst

''Ahmadistische propaganda in Ost Afrika.''
NAMZ, v.14, No.5, 1937: p.148-153.

1022. ------,

''Die quellen der Suaheli Dichtung.'' Der Islam,
v.3, 1942: p.250-268.

1023. ------,

''The tradition of Swahili Islamic poetry.''
Research Bulletin (Centre of Arabic Documenta-
tion, University of Ibadan), v.5, Nos. 1/2,
December 1969: p.21-41.

1024. FITZGERALD, M.L.

''Factors influencing the spread of Islam in
East Africa.'' Orita, v.5, No.2, December 1971:
p.93-104.

1025. FREEMAN-GRENVILLE, G.S.P.

''Islam and Christianity in East Africa before
the mid-nineteenth century.'' African Ecclessiastical Review, v.2, No.3, July 1960: p.193-207.

1026. GARLAKE, Peter S.
The early islamic architecture of the East
African coast. Nairobi & London, Oxford Univ-
ersity Press, 1966. x, 207p. illus., bibliog.

1027. GRIFFITHS, V.L. and SERGEANT, R.B.
Report by the fact-finding mission to study
Muslim education in East Africa. Nairobi, Govt.
Printer, 1958. 23p.

1028. GUTMANN, Br.
''Die Begegnung des Islam mit dem Volkstum der
Ostafrikaner.'' Lutherisches Missionsjahrbuch
(Wallmann, Leipzig), 1930: p.57-71.

1029. HASHIMIYA, Imetunga
''Swahili loflied op de profeet Mohammed: Kaswida
ja miiraji.'' Kongo-Overzee, v.25, Nos. 4/5,
1959: p.170-173.

1030. HARRIES, Lyndon.
''The Arabs and Swahili culture.'' Africa, v.34,
1964: p.224-229.

1031. ------,
Islam in East Africa. London, Universities
Mission to Central Africa, 1924. 92p.

1032. HOLWAY, James D.
''C.M.S. contact with Islam in East Africa
before 1914.'' Journal of Religion in Africa,
v.4, 1971/72: p.200-212.

1033. HOLWAY, James D.
''Islam and Christianity in East Africa.'' In
Barrett, D.B. ed. African initiatives in
religion. 1971: p.262-277.

1034. KARSTEDT, F.O.
''Zur beurteilung des Islam in Deutsch ostafrika.''
Kol Rundschau, 1913: p.728-736.

1035. KNAPPERT, Jan
''The divine names (Arabic and Swahili).''
Swahili, n.s. v.1, No.2, September 1960: p.180-199.

1036. ------,
''Social and moral concepts in Swahili Islamic
literature.'' Africa, v.40, No.2, 1970: p.125-
136, bibliog.
    Sets out the ideas of morality and the
structure of society as reflected in Swahili
Islamic literature. Argues that faith is the
strongest regulating factor in the behaviour of
people in Islamic society.

1037. ------,
''Swahili religious terms.'' Journal of Religion
in Africa, v.3, No.1, 1970: p.67-80.

1038. ------,
Swahili theology in the form of an utenzi. In
Greschat, H.J. (and others) (eds). Wort und
Religion, Stuttgart, 1969: p.282-293.

1039.　MARTIN, B.G.

''Muslim politics and resistance to colonial rule: Shaykh Uways b. Muhammad al-Barawi and the Qadiriya brotherhood in East Africa.'' Journal of African History, v.10, No.3, 1969: p.471-486.

The biographee became a prominent member of the Qadiriya tariqa in Somaliland in about 1870. Until his assassination in 1909 he was involved in education and proselytising from a base in Zanzibar, where he had political support.

1040.　MATHEW, Gervase

''Islamic merchant cities of East Africa.'' Times, 26 June 1951. (Reprint: Colonial Review,) v.7, No.4, December 1951: p.111-112.

1041.　MORRIS, H.S.

''The divine kingship of the Aga Khan: a study of theocracy in East Africa.'' Southwestern Journal of Anthropology, v.14, No.4, Winter 1958: p.454-472.

1042.　PRICE, Thomas

''The Arabs of the Zambezi.'' Muslim World, v.44, 1954.

1043.　REUSCH, R.

Der Islam in Ostafrika mit besonderer Berucksichtigung der mohammedanischen Gebeimorden. Leipzig, A. Klein, 1930.

1044. SACHAU, Eduard
       ''Das gutachten eines muhammedanischen jaristen
       uber die muhammedanischen rechtsverhaltnisse in
       Ostafrika.'' Mitteilungen des Seminars fur
       Orientalische Sprachen (Berlin), v.1, 1898:
       p.1-8.

1045. SCHACHT, Joseph
       ''Notes on Islam in East Africa.'' Studia
       Islamica, v.23, 1965: p.91-136.

1046. TRIMINGHAM, John Spencer
       Islam in East Africa. Oxford, Clarendon Press,
       1964. xii, 198p.

1047. ------,
       ''Islam in East Africa.'' In Africa from early
       times to 1800, edited by P.J.M. McEwan, New York,
       Oxford University Press, 1968: p.343-351.

1048. ------,
       Islam in East Africa; the report of a survey
       undertaken in 1961. 47p. map. (Commission on
       world mission and Evangelism research pamphlets
       no.9).

1049. WATT, William Montgomery
       ''The political relevance of Islam in East
       Africa.'' International Affairs, v.42, 1966:
       p.35-44.

1050. YOUNG, T. Cuyler
       ''East Africa and classical Islam: some remainin<

1050. YOUNG, T. Cuyler (Contd.)

> research problems in relationships.'' <u>Trans-African Journal of History</u>, v.2, No.2, 1972: p.3-10.

ETHIOPIA

1051. ABIR, Mordechai
> <u>Ethiopia: the era of the princes: the challenge of Islam and the reunification of the Christian empire, 1769-1855.</u> Longmans, 1968. xxvi, 208p. illus.
>
> This book is primarily concerned with the development of internal and external trade in Ethiopia, the dissemination of Islam among the Galla, the impact of Egyptian imperialism on Ethiopia, and the expansion and consolidation of Showa.

1052. CERBELLA, Gino
> ''La diffusione in Eritrea della casa musulmana tipica.'' (The spread of the Muslim-type house in Eritrea). <u>Africa</u> (Roma). v.17, No.6, November 1962: p.291-299.

1053. CERULLI, E.
> ''L'Islam en Ethiopie: sa signification histori-que et ses methodes.'' <u>Colloque sur la sociologi</u><u>musulmane</u>. p.317-329.

1054. CERULLI, Enrico.

Islam W. Etiopii (L'Islam en Ethiopie).
Przeglad orientalistyczny (Warsaw), v.1, No.65,
1968: p.3-13.

1055. CRUMMEY, Donald

''Shaikh Zakaryas: an Ethiopian prophet.''
Journal of Ethiopian Studies, v.10, No.1, 1972:
p.55-66.

Bography of a Muslim prophet who became a
major figure in mass conversion to Christianity.

1056. DAVIS, Asa J.

''The sixteenth century jihad in Ethiopia and
its impact on culture.'' Journal of the Historical Society of Nigeria, v.2, No.4, 1963:
p.567-592. v.3, No.1, Dec.,1964: p.113-128.

''The 16th century jihad in Ethiopia was in
a large measure responsible for the greatest
cultural transformation in the history of
Ethiopia.

1057. DEMOZ, Abraham

Moslems and Islam in Ethiopic literature.
Journal of Ethiopian Studies, v.10, No.1, 1972:
p.1-11.

1058. DYE, William McE.

Moslem Egypt and Christian Abyssinia, or military
service under the Khedive, in his provinces and
beyond their borders, as experienced by the
American staff. New York, Negro Universities
Press, 1969. 500p. illus.

1059.   FERRY, Robert
        ''Quelques hypotheses sur les origines des
        conquêtes musulmanes en Abyssinia au xvi^e
        siecle.'' Cahiers d'Etudes Africaines, v.5,
        Nos. 1/2, 1961: p.24-36.

1060.   IWARSSON, J.
        ''Moslem mass movement toward Christianity in
        Abyssinia.'' Moslem World, v.14, July 1924:
        p.286-289.

1061.   MERID, Wolde Aregay
        ''Population movements as a possible factor in
        the Christian-Muslim conflict of medieval
        Ethiopia.'' In Symposium Leo Frobenius, Koln,
        1974, p.266-281.

1062.   MUSTAFA, Z.
        ''The substantive law applied by Muslim courts
        in Ethiopia: possible justifications for the
        continued application of the Sahara.'' Journal
        of Ethiopian law, v.9, No.1, June 1973: p.138-148.

1063.   NERAZZINI, C.
        La conquista musulmana dell'Etiopia nell xvi seco
        Roma, 1891.

1064.   WIET, G.
        ''Les relations egypto-abyssines sous les
        sultans mamlouks.'' Bulletin de la Société d'
        Archeologie Copte, v.4, 1938: p.115-140.

1065.   ZWEMER, Samuel M.
          ''Islam in Ethiopia and Eritrea.'' The Moslem
          World, v.26, No.1, 1936: p.5-15.

1066.   SHACK, William A.
          ''The Masqal-pole: religious conflict and social
          change in Gurageland.'' Africa, v.38, No.4,
          October 1968: p.457-468. bibliog.

1067.   TRIMINGHAM, John Spencer
          Islam in Ethiopia. London, Cass, 1965. 299p.
          A major contribution to the study of Islam
          in Ethiopia, Eritrea and the Somalilands.
          Treats the traditional conflict between Islam
          and Coptic christianity, and concludes that
          whilst Christian expansion is essentially by
          conquest, Islam is by peaceful means.

                              MALAWI

1068.   GREENSTEIN, Robert Carl
          ''A history of Islam in Malawi: Yao and Chewa.''
          Ph.D. Thesis, Syracuse University, 1974.

1069.   HETERWICK, Alexander
          ''Islam and Christianity in Nyasaland.''
          Moslem World, v.17, April 1927: p.184-186.

1070.   HOFMEYER, A.L.
          ''Islam in Nyasaland.'' Moslem World, v.2,
          January 1912: p.3-8.

MALAWI

1071. MACDONALD, Roderick J.
''Religious independency as a means of social advance in Northern Nyasaland in the 1930s.'' Journal of Religions in Africa (Leiden), v.3, No.2, 1970: p.106-129.

KENYA

1072. ANDERSON, James Norman Dalrymple
''Comments (on Kenya Commission reports) with reference to the Muslim community.'' East African Law Journal (Nairobi), v.5, Nos. 1/2, March-June 1969: p.5-20.

1073. BAXTER, P.T.W.
''Acceptance and rejection of Islam among the Boran of the Northern frontier district of Kenya.'' In Islam in Tropical Africa, edited by I.M. Lewis. London, Oxford University Press, 1966: p.233-252.

1074. BERG, F.J. and WALTER, B.J.
''Mosques, population and urban development in Mombasa.'' In Ogot, B.A., (ed). Hadith, 1968: p.47-100.

1075. BUNGER, Robert L.
Islamisation among the Upper Pokome. Syracuse, Program of Eastern African Studies: Syracuse University, 1973. 200p.

192

KENYA

1076. PARKIN, David

''Politics of ritual syncretism: Islam among
the non-Muslim Giriama of Kenya.'' _Africa_,
v.40, No.3, July 1970; p.217-233. Bibliog.

SOMALI

1077. CHEDEVILLE, E.

''Quelques faits de l'organisation sociales
des 'Afar'.'' _Africa_, v.36, 1966: p.173-195.

1078. EBY, Omar

_A whisper in a dry land; a biography of Merlin
Grove, martyr for Muslims in Somalia_. Scottdale,
Pa., Herald Press, 1968.

1079. JARDINE, Douglas James

The Mad Mullah of Somaliland. London, H. Jenkins,
1923. xiv, 336p.

1080. LEWIS, I.M.

''Comformity and contrast in Somali Islam.''
In _Islam in Tropical Africa_, edited by I.M. Lewis.
London, Oxford University Press, 1966: p.253-267.

1081. ------,

''Sufism in Somaliland: a study of tribal Islam.''
_Bulletin of the School of Oriental and African
Studies_, v.27, 1955: p.581-602; v.28, 1956:
p.146-160.

SOMALI

1082. TURTON, E.R.
       ''The impact of Mohammad Abdille Hassan in the
       East African Protectorate.'' Journal of African
       History, v.10, No.4, 1969: p.641-657.

SUDAN

1083. ALLEN, Roland
       ''Islam and Christianity in the Sudan.'' Inter-
       national Review of Missions, v.9, October 1920:
       p.531-543.

1084. ARKELL, Anthony J.
       The history of the Sudan from the earliest times
       to 1821. 2nd ed. New York, Oxford University
       Press, 1961. 282p. illus.

1085. BARCLAY, Harold B.
       ''Muslim 'prophets' in the modern Sudan.''
       Muslim World, v.54, No.4, 1964: p.250-255.
           Account of the proselytising role of two
       muslim prophets, Zayn and Babikr who broke
       away from the familiar and traditional Islamic
       practice.

1086. ------,
       ''Muslim religious practice in a village
       suburb of Khartoum.'' Muslim World, v.53,
       1963: p.205-211.

194

1087.   BASHIR, Mohamed Omer
        ''Abdel Rahman Ibn Hussein el Jabri and his
        book 'History of the Mahdi'.'' Sudan Notes and
        Records, 1963: p.136-139.

1088.   BREVIE, J.
        Islamisme contre naturisme au Soudan francais:
        essai de psychologie de la politique coloniale.
        Paris, Leroux, 1923. xvi, 220p.

1089.   BROWN, Carl
        ''The Sudanese Mahdiya.'' In Rotberg, Robert I.
        and Mazrui, Ali A. Protest and power in black
        Africa. New York, Oxford University Press,
        1970: p.145-168.

1090.   CARDAIRE, Marcel
        L'Islam et le terroir africain; etudes soudanie-
        nnes. Koulouba, Imprimerie du Government, 1954.
        168p. Also in Bulletin de l'IFAN, 1954: p.30-46.

1091.   CASTRIES, H. de
        ''La conquête du Soudan par Moulay Ahmed El
        Mansour.'' Hesperis (Rabat), v.3, 1923: p.433-488.

1092.   CERULLI, Enrico
        ''Christian Nubia, the Baria and the Kunama, in
        the tenth century A.D., according to Ibn Hawqal,
        (Arab geographer).'' Annali dell'Instituto Univ-
        ersitario Orientale di Napoli; v.3, 1949: p.215-
        222.

1093. CLARKE, John H.
''The real story of Khartoum and the Mahdi.''
Negro Digest, February 1967: p.32-36†.

1094. DEHERAIN, H.
''Les Mahdistes sur le Haut-Nil Blanc.'' Comité
des travaux historique et scientifiques. Bulletin,
Section Geographie, v.53, 1938: p.47-62.

1095. DU JARRIC, Gaston
L'état mahdiste du Soudan. Paris, Maisonneuve,
1901.

1096. GRAY, Richard
''Some aspects of Islam in the southern Sudan
during the Turkiya.'' In Northern Africa: Islam
and modernization; papers on the theme of Islamization, modernization, nationalism and independence presented and discussed at a symposium
arranged by the African Studies Association of
the United Kingdom on the occasion of its Annual
General Meeting, 14th September 1971. Edited
with an introduction by Michael Brett. London,
Cass, 1973: p.65-72.

1097. HALLAM, W.K.R.
''The itinerary of Rabih Fadl Allah, 1879-1893.''
Bulletin de l'Institut Fondamental d'Afrique
Noire, v.30, serie B, No.1, 1968: p.165-181.

1098. HASAN, Yusuf Fadl ed.
''External Islamic influences and the progress
of Islamization in the Eastern Sudan between

1098.   HASAN, Yusuf Fadl, ed. (Contd.)

the fifteenth and the nineteenth centuries.''
In Hasan, Y.F. (ed). Sudan in Africa, Khartoum,
1971: p.73-86.

1099.   -------,

''The penetration of Islam in the Eastern Sudan.''
In Islam in Tropical Africa, edited by I.M. Lewis.
London, Oxford University Press, 1966: p.144-159.
Sudan Notes and Records, v.44, 1963: p.1-8.
    The process of Islamization of the Sudan
was accompanied by Arabization which left its
mark on a large part of the country; for Arabic
was not only the language of Islam but also of
trade.

1100.   HILL, Richard
On the frontiers of Islam: two manuscripts
concerning the Sudan under Turco-Egyptian rule
1822-1845. Translated and edited by Richard
Hill. Oxford, Clarendon Press, 1970. 234p.
    This book contains two documents on the
first twenty years of Turco-Egyptian rule in
the Sudan. The first chronicle from 1822-1841
is translated from the Italian, and the second,
from a traveller's diary of 1837 to 1840
translated from the French.

1101.   HOLT, Peter M.
A modern history of the Sudan; from the Funj
Sultanate to the present day. New York,
Praeger, 1961. 255p. illus.

1102.   HOLT, Peter M.
The Mahdist state in the Sudan 1881-1898: a
study of its origins, development and overthrow.
2nd ed. revised and expanded. Oxford, Clarendon
Press, 1970. xv, 295p.

This book describes social and political
conditions in the Egyptian Sudan on the eve of
the Mahdist revolt, analyses the Mahdist idea
and traces the stages by which the Mahdi succeeded
in overthrowing Egyptian administration and
creating a theocratic state in the Sudan.

1103.   ------,
''The sons of Jabir and their kin: a clan of
Sudanese religious notables.'' Bulletin of the
School of Oriental and African Studies, v.30,
No.1, 1967: p.142-157.

The sons of Jabir were eminent religious
teachers in the Nilotic Sudan in the later part
of the 16th century.

1104.   ------,
''Sultan Selim I and the Sudan.'' Journal of
African History, v.8, No.1, 1967: p.19-23.

1105.   HOUDAS, O. and BENOIST, E.
Tarik es Soudan. Histoire du Soudan par Abder-
rahman ben Abdallah et Tonboutki. Paris, E.
Leroux, 1900. 2vols.

1106.   JUREIDINI, L.B.
''The miracles of Ali Dinar of Darfur.'' Muslim
World, v.6, 1900: p.177-209.

1107. KROPACEK, L.

      ''The confrontation of Darfur with the Turco-
      Egyptians.'' Asian and African Studies (Bratis-
      lava), v.6, 1970: p.73-78.

1108. ------,

      ''Title-deeds in the fief system of the Sultanate
      of Darfur.'' Acta Universitatis Carolinae
      (Prague), v.4, 1971: p.33-50.

1109. LIGHTON, G.

      ''The numerical strength of Islam in the Sudan.''
      Moslem World, July 1936: p.253-273.

1110. McCREERY, R.

      ''Moslems and pagans of the Anglo-Egyptian
      Sudan.'' Moslem World, 1946: p.252-260.

1111. MONTEIL, Charles

      ''Notes sur le Tarikh es-Soudan.'' Bulletin de
      l'Institut Fondamental d'Afrique Noire, serie B,
      v.27, 1965: p.479-530.

1112. NADLER, L.F.

      ''The influence of animism in Islam.'' Sudan
      Notes and Records, v.9, No.1, 1926: p.75-87.

1113. O'FAHEY, R.S.

      ''The growth and development of the Keira
      sultanate of Dar Fur.'' Ph.D. Thesis, Univer-
      sity of London, 1972.

1114. O'FAHEY, R.S. and SPAULDING, J.L.
''Hashim and the Musabbaat.'' Bulletin of the
School of Oriental and African Studies, v.35,
1972: p.316-333.

1115. ------,
Kingdoms of the Sudan. London, Methuen, 1974.
235p.
This book is a study of two states, the
Funj Kingdom of Sinnar and the Keira sultanate
of Dar Fur, which form the present day northern
and western regions of Republic of Sudan. The
study is from the sixteenth to the nineteenth
century. Politics, economics, religion form
the main part of the discussion.

1116. OHRWALDER, Joseph
Ten years' captivity in the Mahdi's camp 1882-
1892; from the original manuscripts of Father
Joseph Ohrwalder... by Major F.R. Wingate. 13th
ed. rev. and abridged. London, Low, Matson & Co.,
1893. 471p.

1117. ------,
Aufstand und Reich des Mahdi in Sudan und meine
zehn-jahrige Gefangenschaft dortselbst, Innsbruck,
Rauch, 1892.

1118. PAUL, H.G.B.
''Islam at Uri.'' Sudan Notes and Records, v.35,
1954: p.139-140.

1119.   RANNAT, Muhammad abu

        ''The relationship between Islamic and customary
        law in the Sudan.'' Journal of African Law, v.4,
        1960: p.9-16.

1120.   SADI, Abdurrahman

        Tarikh al Sudan. Translated by Octave Houdas.
        Paris, 1964. (Publications de l'Ecole des Langues
        Orientales Vivantes, series 4).

1121.   SHAKED, Haim

        ''A manuscript biography of the Sudanese Mahdi.''
        Bulletin of the School of Oriental and African
        Studies, v.32, No.3, 1969: p.527-540.

1122.   SMITH, V. Mitchell

        ''Tarikh es-Soudan and Tarikh al-Fattach.''
        (translated from Fench and Arabic) Unpublished
        Ph.D. dissertation, Department of History,
        Texas Technological College, 1967.

1123.   SPAULDING, J.L.

        ''Kings of Sun and Shadow: a history of the
        Abdullab provinces of the northern Sinnar
        sultanate, 1500-1800.'' Ph.D. Thesis, Columbia
        University, 1971.

1124.   STEVENSON, R.C.

        ''Some aspects of the spread of Islam in the
        Nuba mountains (Kordofan) Province, Republic
        of the Sudan.'' In Islam in Tropical Africa,
        edited by I.M. Lewis, London, Oxford University
        Press, 1966: p.208-231. Sudan Notes and Records,

1124. STEVENSON, R.C. (Contd.)

v.44, 1963: p.9-20.

1125. THEOBALD, A.B.

The Mahdiya: a history of the Anglo-Egyptian Sudan, 1881-1899. London, Longmans, 1951. 273p.

'126. ''THREE impressions of Khartoum during the Turkiya (from the letters and diaries of Italian missionaries.'' Sudan Notes, v.41, 1960: p.101-106.

These impressions were collected from three letters written in 1842 by Father Luigi Montuori, 1853 by Father G. Beltrame and 1881 by Father B. Rolleri.

1127. TRAORE, D.

''Makanta Djigui, fondateur de la magie soudanaise.'' Notes Africaines, No.35, 1947: p.23-27.

1128. TRIMINGHAM, John Spencer

The Christian approach to Islam in the Sudan. London, Oxford University Press, 1948. 73p.

1129. ------,

Islam in the Sudan. London, Frank Cass, 1965. x, 280p. illus.

An expert treatise on the practices of Islam in the Sudan, with competent accounts on the geographic, ethnographic and historical factors.

1130. VOLL, John

''Effects at Islamic structures on modern Islamic

SUDAN

1130.   VOLL, John (Contd.)

expansion in the Eastern Sudan.'' <u>International</u>
<u>Journal of African Historical Studies</u>, v.7, No.1,
1974: p.85-98.

1131.   WATSON, A.

''Islam in Egypt and Sudan.'' <u>Missionary Review</u>
<u>of the World</u>, v.30, May 1907: p.351-358.

1132.   WESTERMANN, D.

''Islam in the Eastern Sudan.'' <u>International</u>
<u>Review of Missions</u>, July 1913: p.454-485.

1133.   WINGATE, <u>Sir</u> Francis Reginald

<u>Mahdiism and the Egyptian Sudan: being an account</u>
<u>of the rise and progress of Mahdiism and of</u>
<u>subsequent events in the Sudan to the present</u>
<u>time</u>.   London, New York, Macmillan, 1891. 617p.

TANZANIA

1134.   CONFERENCE ON MUSLIM EDUCATION. Dar-es-Salaam, 1959.

<u>Proceedings of the Conference on Muslim education</u>
<u>held in Dar-es-Salaam on 20th-22nd November, 1958</u>.
Nairobi, East African High Command, 1958. 40p.

1135.   FREEMAN-GRENVILLE, G.S.P.

''Some preliminary observations on medieval
mosques near Dar-es-Salaam.'' <u>Tanganyika Notes</u>,
v.36, January 1954: p.64-70. illus.

203

1136.   LIENHARDT, Peter
        ''A controversy over Islamic custom in Kilwa
        Kivinje, Tanzania.'' In <u>Islam in Tropical
        Africa</u>, edited by I.M. Lewis, London, Oxford
        University Press, 1966: p.374-386.

1137.   ------,
        ''The Mosque college of Lamu and its social
        background.'' <u>Tanganyika Notes</u>, v.53, October
        1959: p.228-242.

1138.   TANNER, Ralph E.S.
        ''The relationship between the sexes in a
        coastal Islamic society, Pagani District, Tan-
        ganyika.'' <u>African Studies</u>, v.21, No.2, 1962:
        p.70-82.
        Three factors influencing the hetero-sexual
        relations of the Swahili-speaking peoples of
        Pagani are industrialization, infertility and
        Islam. These factors tend to make members of
        opposite sexes contemptuous of each other.

UGANDA

1139.   BAMUNOBA, J.
        ''Notes on Islam in Ankole.'' <u>Dini na Mila</u>,
        No.2, 1965: p.5-17.

1140.   BYRNE, Hubert J.
        ''Muslim education in Uganda.'' <u>African World</u>,
        April 1960: p.11-12.

1141. CARTER, Felice
          ''The education of African Muslims in Uganda.''
          Uganda Journal, v.29, No.2, 1965: p.193-199.
             Historical sketch of the growth of Muslim
          schools in Uganda.

1142. ————,
          ''Muslim education in Uganda.'' Uganda Journal,
          v.29. 1965: p.193-198.

1143. FITZGERALD, M.L.
          ''Religious education among muslims in Uganda.''
          In Geoffrey N. Brown and Mervin Hiskett. Conflict
          and harmony in education in tropical Africa.
          London, Allen & Unwin, 1975: p.200-211.

1144. ——————,
          ''Some notes on the religious education of
          Muslims in Uganda.'' Uganda Journal, v.35, No.2,
          1971: p.215-218.

1145. GEE, T.W.
          ''A century of Muhammadan influence in Buganda,
          1852-1951.'' Uganda Journal, v.22, No.2, September
          1958: p.139-150. illus.

1146. GRAY, J.M.
          ''Ahmad B. Ibraihim; the first Arab to reach
          Buganda.'' Uganda Journal, v.11, 1947: p.80-97.

1147. KASOZI, A.B.K.
          ''The impact of Koran school on the education
          of African Muslims in Uganda, 1900-1968.''

1147. KASOZI, A.B.K. (Contd.)

Dini na Mila, v.4, No.2, 1970: p.1-21.

1148. ------,

The spread of Islam in Uganda; a seminar paper
presented in the Department of History, Makerere
University, Kampala, November 1969.

1149. KATAMBA, Ahmed and WELBOURN, F.B.
''Muslim martyrs of Buganda.'' Uganda Journal,
v.28, No.2, September 1964: p.151-163.

1150. KESBY, John D.
''The Warangi: Muslim traditionalists, Catholic
progressives?'' Proceedings of East African
Institute of Social Research. Conference,
Kampala, January 1966. 8p.

1151. MIDDLETON, J.
''The Yakan or Allah water cult among the Lugbara.
Royal Anthropological Institute Journal, v.93,
January-June 1963: p.80-108.

1152. ODED, Arye
Islam in Uganda: islamization through a centra-
lized state in pre-colonial Africa. London,
Halsted Press, New York, Israel Universities
Press, 1974. 381p. bibliog.

1153. RIGBY, P.J.A.
''Sociological factors in the contact of the
Gogo of Central Tanzania with Islam.'' In Islam

1153.   RIGBY, P.J.A. (Contd.)

in Tropical Africa, edited by I.M. Lewis.
London, Oxford University Press, 1966: p.268-295.

1154.   SOLZBACHER, Regina M.
Continuity through change in the social history
of Kibuli (Muslim community). Uganda Journal,
v.33, No.2, 1969: p.163-174.

1155.   SYKES, J.
''A further note on the education of African
Muslims.'' Uganda Journal, v.30, No.2, 1966:
p.227-228.

1156.   TWADDLE, Michael
''The Muslim revolution in Buganda.'' African
Affairs, v.71, No.282, January 1972: p.54-72.

MADAGASCAR

1157.   ARDANT DU PICQ, Col.
L'influence islamique sur une population maḻayo-
polynesienne de Madagascar. Paris, Lavauzelle,
1935.

1158.   FERRAND, G.
Les Musulmans à Madagascar et aux îles Comores.
Paris, Leroux, 1891-1903. 3vols.
An important work on the Muslims of the
Madagascar by a leading authority.

MADAGASCAR

1159. POIRIER, Charles
''Terre d'Islam en mer Malgache.'' Bulletin de
l'Academie Malgache, v.32, (no. special du
cinquantenaire), 1954: p.72-116. illus.

1160. RUSILLON, Henry
''Islam in Madagascar.'' Moslem World, v.12,
1922: p.286-289.

1161. WALKER, John
''Islam in Madagascar.'' The Moslem World,
v.22, No.4, 1932: p.393-397.

1162. ZWEMER, Samuel M.
''Islam in Madagascar.'' Moslem World, April
1940: p.151-167.

MOCAMBIQUE

1163. PEIRONE, Frederico J.
''A importancia do estudo da lingua e da cultura
arabe para a missionacao dos indigenas islamizados
de Mocambique.'' Garcia de Orta, (Lisboa), v.4,
No.3, 1956: p.371-381.

SOUTH AFRICA

1164. GARDENER, G.D.A.
''Mohamedanism in South Africa.'' South African
Quarterly, v.1, December 1914: p.53-56.

1165.   HAMPSON, A.R.
            ''Moslems in Cape town.'' Moslem World, July
            1934: p.271-277.

1166.   ROCHLIN, S.A.
            ''Aspects of Islam in nineteenth-century South
            Africa.'' Bulletin of the School of Oriental
            and African Studies, v.10, No.1, 1939: p.213-221.

1167.   SMITH, G.R.
            ''A Muslim saint in South Africa.'' African
            Studies, v.28, No.4, 1969: p.267-278. illus.
                 A detailed biographical study of Sufi Sahib,
            alias Shah Ghulam Muhammad Habibi, a mystic of
            the Chisti order whose arrival in Durham from
            India opened up a chapter of some importance
            and significance in the history of Islam in
            South Africa.

1168.   ZWEMER, Samuel M.
            ''Islam at Capetown.'' Moslem World, October
            1925: p.327-333.

1169.   ------,
            ''Moslem menace in South Africa.'' Missionary
            Review of the World, v.37, October 1914:
            p.733-738.

1170.   ------,
            ''A survey of Islam in South Africa.''
            International Review of Missions, October
            1925: p.73-91.

INDEX

INDEX

Sachau, Eduard, 1044

Sadi, Abdurrahman, 1120

Sadler, George W., 793

Sainte-Croix, F.W. de, 794

Saint-Martin, Yves, 795-796, 920-922

Saint-Pere, 578

Salih, Muhammad, 797

Salloun, D., 197

Samb, Amar, 198, 798-799, 923-926

Samb, Majhetar, 199

Sanneh, L.O., 200, 515

Sauvaget, J., 963-964

Sayers, Eldred F., 571

Schacht, Joseph, 201-202, 413, 1045

Schieffelin, Henry Maunsell, 327

Schoy, S., 203

Schrader, L. Maro-
    see
    Maro-Schrader, L.

Schultze, Arnold, 328, 800

Schwerin, Hans Hugold, 204

Sciou, Chef de bataillon, 331

Seetzen, M. de·
    see
    De Seetzen, M.

Seidel, H., 414

Sell, E., 329

Semonin, P., 437

Sergeant, R.B., 1027

Sesay, S.I., 952

Shack, William A., 1066

Shaked, Haim, 1121

Shani, Ma'aji Isa, 801

Shelton, A.S., 629

Sheppard, Roscoe Burton, 330

Shepperson, George, 974

al-Shinqiti, Ahmad Ibn al-Amin, 650

Shoemaker, Michael Myers, 205

Shorter encyclopaedia of Islam, 67

Sidibe, M., 630

Sidiki, Abdulai, 547

Silla, O., 415

Skinner, Elliot P., 965-967

Smith, G.R., 1167

Smith, H.F.C., 68-72, 496, 802-813

Smith, M.G., 814-815

Smith, V. Mitchell, 1122

Soh, Sire Abbas, 928

Solken, Heinz, 548

Solzbacher, Regina M., 1154

Sourdel, Dominique, 206

Sow, Alfa Ibrahim, 579

Spaulding, J.L., 1114-1115, 1123

Stenning, D.J., 816

Stepniewska, Barbara, 416-417

Stern, S.M., 73, 145

Stevens, Phyllis, 549

Stevenson, R.C., 1124

Stewart, C.C., 74, 497, 550, 651-654

Stewart, E.K., 654

Stoddard, Theodore L., 207